A Friendly Guide to PAUL

Christopher J. Monaghan

garratt PUBLISHING

Published in Australia by
Garratt Publishing
32 Glenvale Crescent
Mulgrave, Vic. 3170

www.garrattpublishing.com.au

Copyright © Christopher J. Monaghan 2014

All rights reserved. Except as provided by the Australian copyright law,
no part of this book may be reproduced in any way without
permission in writing from the publisher.

Design by Lynne Muir

Images: www.thinkstock.com, Lynne Muir and Rosanna Morales
p.14, Conversion of Saint Paul, Caravaggio (Merisi, Michelangelo da (1571-1610) Church of Santa Maria del Popolo, Rome © 2012. Photo Scala, Florence

Scripture quotations are drawn from the New Revised Standard Version of the Bible, copyright © 1989 by the Division of Christian Education of the National Council of the Churches of Christ in the USA. Used by permission.

All rights reserved.

Nihil Obstat: Monsignor Greg Bennet MA (Oxon), LSS, D.Theol
Diocesan Censor

Imprimatur: Archbishop Denis Hart DD
Archbishop of Melbourne
Date: 21 September 2013

The Nihil Obstat and Imprimatur are official declarations that a book or pamphlet is free of doctrinal or moral error. No implication is contained therein that those who have granted the Nihil Obstat and Imprimatur agree with the contents, opinions or statements expressed. They do not necessarily signify that the work is approved as a basic text for catechetical instruction.

9781921946998

Cataloguing in Publication information for this title is available from the National Library of Australia.
www.nla.gov.au

Every effort has been made to race the original source of copyright material contained in this book. The publisher would be pleased to hear from copyright holders to rectify any errors or omissions.

CONTENTS

INTRODUCTION   3

PAUL'S BACKGROUND   7
   The Cities of Paul   8
   The Journeys of Paul   9
   Chronology   10

PAUL'S MISSIONARY JOURNEYS   12
   Paul's Conversion   14
   Physical Description of Paul   16
   How Many Letters did Paul Write?   17
   Household Churches   18
   Paul and his Co-Workers   21
   Getting a Handle on Paul's Thoughts:
   Some Key Pauline Concepts   22
   Paul and Community   28
   The Importance of Women in the Pauline Communities   29

THE LETTERS OF PAUL   31

SOME RECOMMENDED READING   48

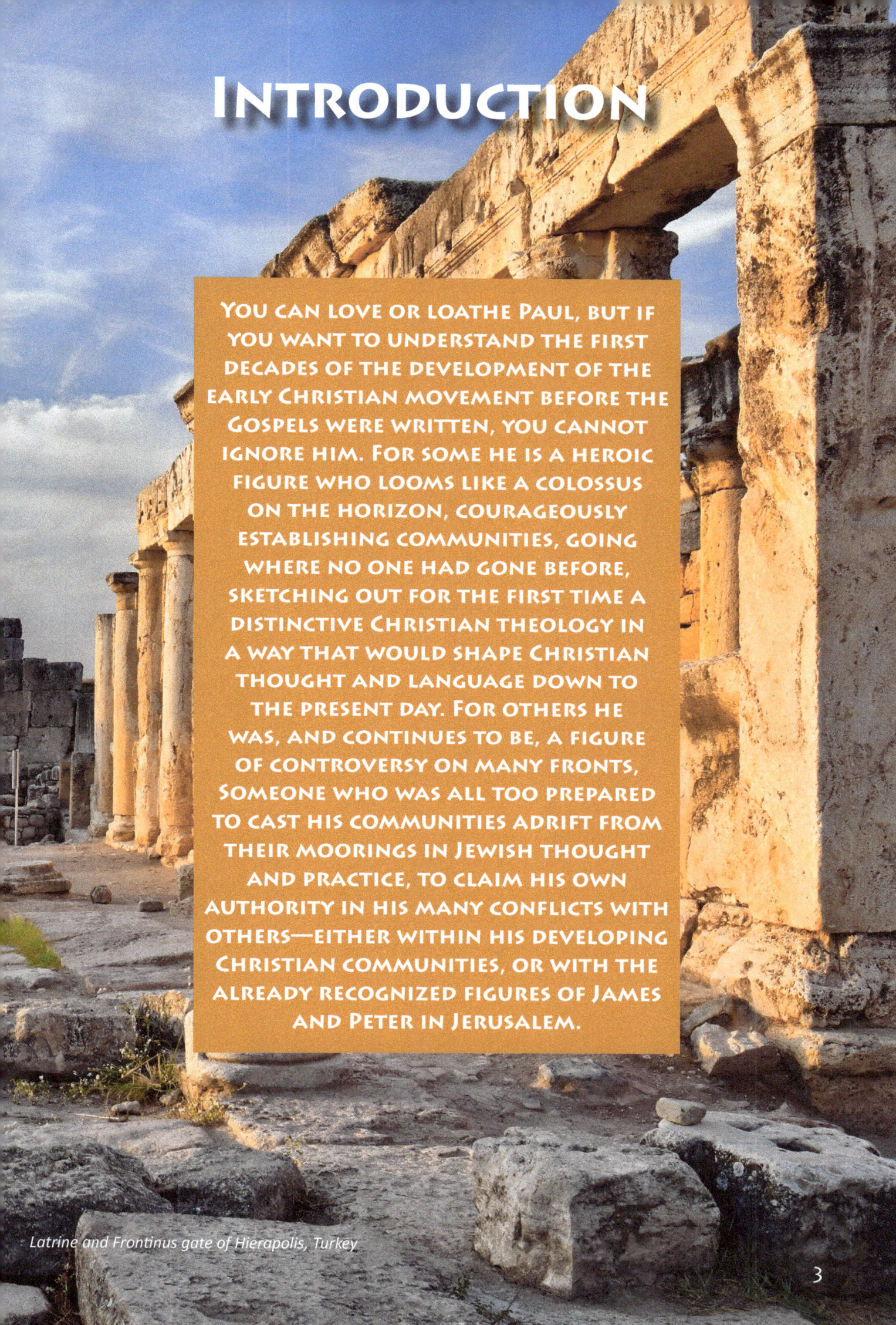

Introduction

You can love or loathe Paul, but if you want to understand the first decades of the development of the early Christian movement before the Gospels were written, you cannot ignore him. For some he is a heroic figure who looms like a colossus on the horizon, courageously establishing communities, going where no one had gone before, sketching out for the first time a distinctive Christian theology in a way that would shape Christian thought and language down to the present day. For others he was, and continues to be, a figure of controversy on many fronts, someone who was all too prepared to cast his communities adrift from their moorings in Jewish thought and practice, to claim his own authority in his many conflicts with others—either within his developing Christian communities, or with the already recognized figures of James and Peter in Jerusalem.

Latrine and Frontinus gate of Hierapolis, Turkey

> ¹If I speak in the tongues of mortals and of angels, but do not have love, I am a noisy gong or a clanging cymbal. ² And if I have prophetic powers, and understand all mysteries and all knowledge, and if I have all faith, so as to remove mountains, but do not have love, I am nothing. ³ If I give away all my possessions, and if I hand over my body so that I may boast,e but do not have love, I gain nothing.
> ⁴ Love is patient; love is kind; love is not envious or boastful or arrogant ⁵ or rude. It does not insist on its own way; it is not irritable or resentful; ⁶ it does not rejoice in wrongdoing, but rejoices in the truth. ⁷ It bears all things, believes all things, hopes all things, endures all things. ⁸ Love never ends. But as for prophecies, they will come to an end; as for tongues, they will cease; as for knowledge, it will come to an end. ⁹ For we know only in part, and we prophesy only in part; ¹⁰ but when the complete comes, the partial will come to an end. ¹¹ When I was a child, I spoke like a child, I thought like a child, I reasoned like a child; when I became an adult, I put an end to childish ways. ¹² For now we see in a mirror, dimly, but then we will see face to face. Now I know only in part; then I will know fully, even as I have been fully known. ¹³ And now faith, hope, and love abide, these three; and the greatest of these is love.
>
> 1 Cor 13:1–13

Given that this work is intended to be a friendly guide to Paul it's important to state at the outset how this is to be understood. This does not so much indicate that the guide is one that will take a stance that is always friendly to Paul in the sense of defending him, so much as being a guide that sets out to be friendly to you, the modern reader of his letters. Week after week we are invited to make sense of Paul's writings in our cycle of readings, and often the modern reader laments that his letters are difficult to understand!

If you have ever voiced such an opinion be of good cheer: even in the first century the author of 2 Peter was known to observe *'There are some things in them hard to understand, which the ignorant and unstable twist to their own destruction, as they do the other scriptures.'* (2 Pet 3:16) Whether the author meant writings or scriptures is open to debate, but what concerns us here is that, even then, Paul's thought was not easy to understand, even if his writings were already starting to be collected and preserved.

There are a number of reasons why the modern reader should experience some perplexity when reading the letters of Paul, and they are worth outlining. For a start, these letters were not written in English, but a dialect of Greek current in the Roman empire of Paul's time called Koine. Paul, like his writings, are works of a particular time; written from, and addressed to, a religious and social context that is not our own. It almost seems too simple a point to make, but it is one that our constant exposure to the letters of Paul as Christians tends to obscure. There is the danger of thinking just because we have heard or read these letters from childhood we should have some natural capacity to follow their logic, understand the concepts, and then be moved to implement Paul's instructions. To be sure, there is a great deal in these letters that transcend the boundaries of time and place and culture. 1 Cor 13:1–13, with its description of love, is but one sublime example. On the other hand, there are many texts that demand a great deal more work on the part of the reader and for a number of reasons.

The ways that Paul expresses himself have been shaped by his context. In particular, he expresses himself in the categories of a first century diaspora Jew who grows up immersed in Greek culture and living in the context of the Roman Empire.

So far so good, and I can hear some of you thinking, 'What's the big deal?' Without wanting to labour the point: this is but the tip of the iceberg. Unless we understand something of the world of Paul we are not actually listening to Paul at all, but some other 'construct' of him.

We learn best by examples, so let's begin with the claim that Paul says some very unflattering things about his various opponents from time to time. In Corinth there was a group of Christians who had come to Corinth after Paul and his co-workers had established this predominately Gentile community that gathered in various household churches. They claimed that they had letters of recommendation from Jerusalem. It seems

they claimed that they were more authentically Jewish Christians than Paul himself. Responding to them, Paul claims that they are '... *false apostles, deceitful workers, disguising themselves as apostles of Christ.*'(2 Cor 11:13)

From our perspective it is understandable that we cringe at the way these probably well-intentioned disciples are caricatured and their reputation maligned by Paul. From a cultural perspective we need to appreciate that Paul and his contemporaries lived in an honour and shame society in which every challenge to one's honour was expected to be defended; otherwise, one would be conceding the claims of one's opponents. His honour had been challenged, and he was within his rights—his honour in fact demanded that he defend himself by doubting the true motivations of his accusers.

This one example has many applications: Paul's world is not our world, and his letters are not written for us, even though our Christian life has been shaped by them. There is a famous cartoon of Charles Shultz where Linus reflects on Paul's letters after returning from Sunday school: 'I MUST ADMIT, IT MAKES ME FEEL A LITTLE GUILTY.... I ALWAYS FEEL LIKE I'M READING SOMEONE'S MAIL!' This is exactly the point. It is someone else's mail; we are listening in on a conversation between Paul and his converts that was never intended for us. One cannot help but wonder what Paul would have thought knowing that two thousand years later his letters addressed to the communities of Corinth, Galatia, Macedonia and Rome would still be closely read and examined.

Another factor to keep in mind is that not only are we listening to someone else's conversation, we also run the risk of not having access to the interpretation of the letter that the recipients of the letters had. Some of the unsung heroes and heroines of the **Pauline communities** were those who first read and explained the letters on Paul's behalf. Imagine the

A colonnaded street in Turkey

Pauline communities

It is customary to speak of the communities founded by Paul and his co-workers as Pauline communities. It is worth considering what we mean by 'Pauline.' The communities that were founded by Paul and his co-workers represented a certain style of Christianity in terms of their practice and attitudes. While we may think of early Christianity as a single movement it would be more accurate to think of a number of communities and house churches - some predominately Jewish in thought and practice, others Gentile, and others mixed communities of Jews and Gentiles. The communities established by Paul were deeply indebted, as Paul himself was, to the Jewish tradition, but circumcision and obedience to all the precepts of the Jewish Law were not required to become a member of the Christian community.

From Paul's perspective we can see that he saw the communities in some sense as his own. He speaks of betrothing them to Christ (2 Cor 11:2), and he expected their loyalty to the message he first preached to them, as he preached it to them (Gal 1:8-9). He saw himself as having an ongoing relationship with them as founder, apostle and guide (1 Cor 4:15).

diplomatic and communication skills required by the person entrusted to challenge those Corinthians who were supporting a fellow Christian involved in an incestuous relationship (1 Cor 5), or those rich members who saw no problem with being drunk when the poorer members of the community came to partake in the Eucharistic celebration!(1 Cor 11:21)

Paul's letters were often written in response to problems that either Paul or members within the various communities had identified. For instance, Philemon was written to help a Christian slave (Onesimus) who had fled to Paul during one of his imprisonments. Its aim is ensuring a fraternal homecoming from his Christian master, Philemon. In order to understand such a letter, background information regarding the period is needed on such matters as the rights of slaves and masters, the ways in which Christian households were organised, the rights of Paul as friend and apostle to demand anything of Philemon, and the rights of a master over his slave.

We are fortunate indeed that the house churches in Corinth were at odds with each other and with Paul, otherwise Paul's teaching on the scandal of the cross in 1 Cor 1–2 might have been lost to us: not because he would not have had the understanding, but that it would not have been preserved in a written form. If they had not been so caught up in competition with one another in terms of how the gift of tongues was to be used and appreciated within the community then his great commentary on love in 1 Cor 13 might never have been written.

Our communication is always shaped by our context and Paul is no exception. Paul's patterns of speech, the examples he uses, the ways that his arguments are expressed have all been shaped by his religious upbringing as a devout Pharisaic Jew, and by the religious and philosophical thought of the Greco-Roman world. Again, this might seem self-evident but I continue to be amazed at how quickly this is forgotten when people start to read Paul's letters. He uses the normal and well-known rhetorical practices of his time to convince his readers of a certain attitude or course of action.

These practices included: *deliberative rhetoric*, which was concerned with convincing people to choose a certain course of action; *forensic rhetoric*, the rhetoric of the law courts determining a person's guilt or innocence; and *ceremonial rhetoric*, used to honour people in life or in death. In Paul's letters these kinds of rhetoric abound, and are further enriched by Paul's use of Jewish forms of rhetoric, particularly in his use of the scriptures. The point being made here is that modern readers often have difficulty in following Paul's line of argument in certain passages, or letters e.g. The letter to the Galatians. This should not surprise us because we are listening to a style of persuasive communication that first century Christians of the Greco-Roman world were familiar with—the customary ways of communicating they all understood. So if we wish to understand Paul better, we need to take some time to become familiar with them to.

Paul's Background

One of the reasons underlying the success of Paul's missionary activity was that he was a devout and jealous Pharisaic Jew who grew up in Tarsus in the Roman province of Cilicia. His mission in Syria, Asia Minor, Macedonia, Achaia and Rome would rely for its success not only on his conviction, commitment and enthusiasm, but also on the fact that he was a person in which worlds and cultures met. The Greek dialect that he spoke functioned much as English does today. Geographically he was not from the heart of the Roman Empire, even though he was a citizen, and from a religious perspective he was not from Jerusalem, even though he was a devout Pharisee.

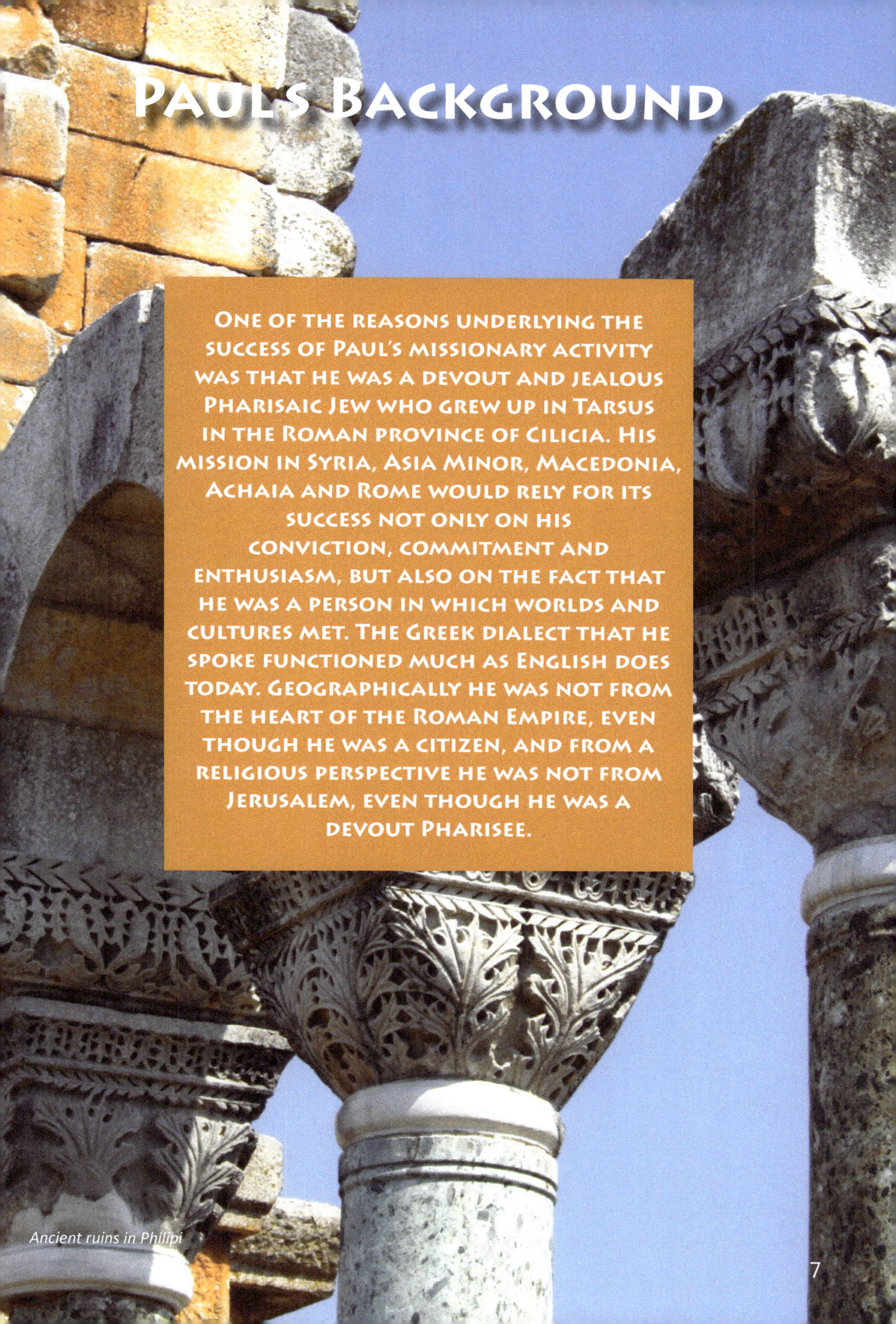

Ancient ruins in Philipi

The Cities of Paul

One of the things that can be learned from the letters is that Paul lost no time in trying to spread the Good News of Jesus as far as he possibly could before the return of the Lord. He writes in Rom 10:14 'But how are they to call on one in whom they have not believed? And how are they to believe in one of whom they have never heard? And how are they to hear without someone to proclaim him?'

The letters attest to a missionary strategy that involved going to as many major cities as possible, by sea and by foot—making use of the well-established system of Roman roads. Paul and his co-workers targeted major population centres, especially those that were strategically placed to serve as a base for ongoing missionary endeavours. Cities such as Philippi and Thessalonica were situated on the *Via Egnatia*, the major link between the Adriatic and Byzantium (later Constantinople).

Corinth's location was such that this cosmopolitan city controlled trade and travel between southern and northern Greece by sea or road. Ephesus was the capital for Asia Minor and was accessible by sea or road. Even at the time of writing Romans, Paul's intention is to move on to new mission opportunities in Spain.(Rom 15:24) Because he is so committed to establish new communities, he expresses great frustration with those who seem to take advantage of the communities he has already established, without taking the risk of starting their own. His aim is to keep moving on 'so that we may proclaim the good news in lands beyond you, without boasting of work already done in someone else's sphere of action.'(2 Cor 10:16)

During this dynamic time of expansion, what is clear is that the Pauline communities were largely urban and, while they were Greek speaking, they were cities of the Roman Empire: as such they were diverse culturally and religiously. Such diversity was both a blessing and a challenge, and the letters attest to the many issues that arose while these early Christian communities were developing, issues that sometimes called for great creativity.

An ancient chapel in Crete

The Journeys of Paul

While we are used to thinking in terms of four journeys undertaken by Paul, this is largely Luke's reconstruction of Paul's ministry written some twenty years or more after Paul had died. This is not to say that Luke's portrayal in Acts of the Apostles doesn't contain a good deal of reliable information, but it has been coloured to some degree by Luke's own narrative agenda and concerns in describing the expansion of the early Christian communities in an orderly fashion.(cf. Luke 1:1–4) It has been said if Paul was asked what missionary journey he was on he wouldn't have been able to tell you!

This doesn't mean that Paul didn't undertake many journeys as an apostle—far from it—it is more a matter of knowing that our picture is always going to be incomplete. It is incomplete because Paul saw no reason to keep a diary of his travels. In 2 Cor 11:22–29 there is a catalogue of the many dangers Paul faced on the road, such as shipwrecks, beatings, robbery, imprisonment, Jewish and Roman punishments. Galatians 1–2 provides a picture written after some seventeen years of ministry in which certain elements are well outlined: his initial ministry in Damascus, going to Jerusalem after three years to meet Peter, returning to Jerusalem after fourteen years of ministry, and confronting Peter in Antioch. The letters indicate that there was an intense period of activity when he was involved in not only preaching the Gospel and the care of communities, but also the collection for the poor in Jerusalem that involved the churches of Corinth, Macedonia and Rome. When Paul writes to the community of Rome he intends to receive assistance from them and extend his mission as far as Spain. Paul mentions in Rom 15:19 that he had preached the Gospel from Jerusalem to Illyricum! There is a clearly expressed sense of pride that he has not spared any effort to preach the Gospel and establish as many communities as possible before the return of the Lord. (cf. Romans 10:15)

Given his efforts, it is understandable that he expresses some sense of frustration with other missionaries who, from Paul's perspective, take advantage of the base that he has established, without going to new cities and establishing communities where the Gospel message had not been preached before.(2 Cor 10:14–16)

The letters of Paul attest the fact that there was a considerable amount of movement, and that it was not isolated to Paul and his co-workers. Letters were sent by Paul to his communities with trusted co-workers like Timothy and Titus. Community members such as Chloe's people (1 Cor 1:11), who came from Corinth to Ephesus, creatively combined their business travel with opportunities to pass on news and ask Paul's advice. The letters witness to Paul's efforts to ensure that wandering missionaries would receive a warm welcome as they moved from one community to another. (cf. 1 Cor 16:10; Rom 16:1–2)

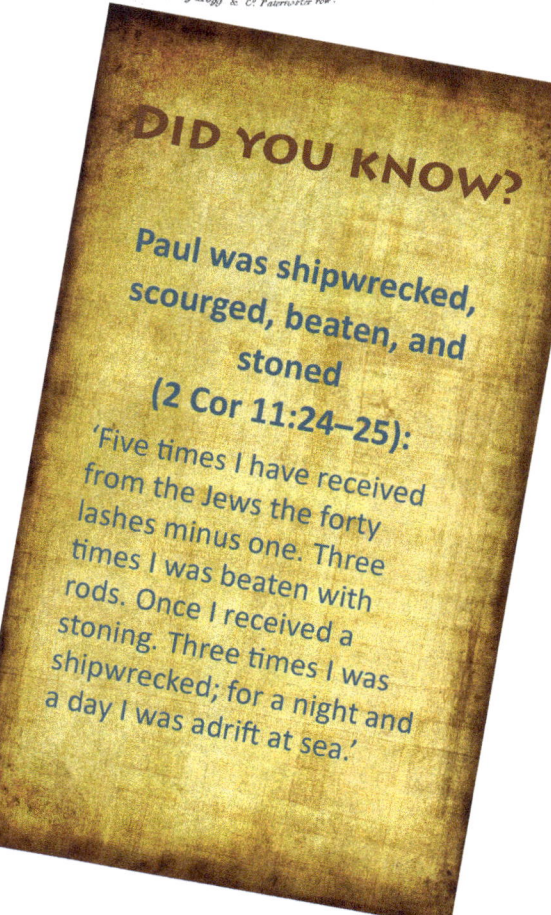

Did you know?

Paul was shipwrecked, scourged, beaten, and stoned (2 Cor 11:24–25):

'Five times I have received from the Jews the forty lashes minus one. Three times I was beaten with rods. Once I received a stoning. Three times I was shipwrecked; for a night and a day I was adrift at sea.'

9

Chronology

Our picture of Paul is a composite one, pieced together from Luke's portrayal of Paul's life and ministry in Acts of the Apostles—written some twenty years after Paul's death—and what we can learn from his letters themselves. As a rule of thumb, whenever there is any conflict between the two sets of information, precedence has to be given to Paul's own words, especially the sequence he provides in Gal 1:11–2:14. Much as we would like it, we have no indication from the letters as to his age when converted, although Acts 7:58 introduces Paul into the narrative as a young man named Saul at the death of Stephen. There is probably no reason to doubt this particular detail, though it is itself imprecise.

As far as external dates are concerned, there is the reference in 2 Cor 11:32 to King Aretas of Damascus who tried to capture him. This would have occurred somewhere around 37–39 CE. This means that the latest that Paul can have begun his apostolic mission is within ten years of the death of Jesus. When writing his letters, Paul was not concerned with giving a blow-by-blow description of his ministry, he was living his life rather than describing it for posterity. As a consequence there will always be gaps in the information that can be gleaned from the letters. Acts makes mention of certain details that can be of assistance in placing Paul's ministry within a framework of external events and people. Acts mentions the time of Gallio as proconsul in Corinth 51–52 CE (Acts 18:12), a famine in Judea (Acts 7:11), Festus' arrival in Caesaria (Acts 25:1,6,13,23) around 55–60 CE, and the edict of Claudius in around 40–49 CE.(Acts 18:2) These details have to be used carefully, but they clearly show Luke's efforts to place Paul within his contemporary world.

John Knox suggested the following chronology:

An ancient road in Philippi

Pauline Chronology

TRADITIONAL	EVENT	REVISIONIST
AD 36	Conversion to Christ	AD 30/34
39	Visit to Jerusalem after Damascus	33/37
40–44	In Cilicia	After 37
44–45	At Antioch	
46–49	(First) Missionary Journey, beginning in Antioch, to Cyprus and southern Asia Minor, returning to Antioch	After 37
	(Second) Missionary Journey, beginning in Antioch, through southern Asia Minor to N. Galatia, Macedonia, CORINTH (I Thess), return to Jerusalem and Antioch	39–41/43 (41–43)
49	Jerusalem conference	47/51
50–52	(Second) Missionary Journey, beginning in Antioch, through southern Asia Minor to N. Galatia, Macedonia, CORINTH (I Thess), return to Jerusalem and Antioch	see above
54–58	(Third) Missionary Journey, beginning in Antioch, through N. Galatia to EPHESUS; three-year stay there—imprisoned? (Gal, Phil, Phlm, I Cor)	indistinct from second (48/55)
	Paul goes through Macedonia toward Corinth (II Cor, Gal?), winters at CORINTH (Rom), returns to Jerusalem	(after 54)
58–60	Arrested in Jerusalem; imprisoned two years in Caesarea (Phil?)	52–55 or 56–58
60–61	Sent to ROME; long sea journey	
61–63	Prisoner in ROME for two years (Phil? Phlm?)	
after summer 64	Death in Rome under Nero	

Table from: *AN INTRODUCTION TO THE NEW TESTAMENT,* Raymond E. Brown S.S., Doubleday, 1977.

Paul's Conversion?

It might come as a surprise to learn that the conversion of Paul is a much debated conversation topic among Pauline scholars. No one would dispute that this encounter between Saul of Tarsus and the Risen Lord would cause him to radically change his life and direction. What is debated is more a matter of whether this radical shift should be called a conversion. The point at issue is whether Paul changed from one religion to another, that is, from Judaism to Christianity, or whether he simply came to see God's promises of a Messiah to Israel to now be fulfilled in the crucified and risen Jesus of Nazareth.

Nazarene heresy

It can come as something of a shock for contemporary Christians to talk about the early Christian movement as the Nazarene heresy, but that is how it was considered by Paul, and those who commissioned him to eradicate belief in Jesus of Nazareth. For them, belief in Jesus as the promised Messiah was at the very least mistaken, and at worst it was a belief that threatened the unity and integrity of the Jewish community. Paul's own response to the Christian movement was that of decisive action to gather believers and bring them before Jewish authorities to confront them with the error of their ways. They were forced to either abandon their mistaken belief in Jesus, or face punishment. The New Testament mentions on numerous occasions that Christians needed to prepare themselves for rejection and being brought before Synagogues and other authorities, both religious and civil, on account of their belief in Jesus as the promised Messiah.(Mark 4:17; 10:30; Matt 10:17-18,23)

Caravaggio (1571–1610): Conversion of Saint Paul. *Rome, Church of Santa Maria del Popolo.*

It needs to be understood that Paul may not have seen the point of our question—he was a Jew and remained so all his life—but his encounter with the Risen one led him to recast his appreciation of his own rich tradition. One of the points that Paul highlights is that the encounter with the Risen Lord was accompanied by a clear sense of mission to the Gentiles. This good news of Jesus was to be shared with all humanity, and it is here that he came into conflict with other early Christian leaders who would have shared in Paul's vision of God's saving plan for all humanity, but would have differed in terms of how that would manifest itself in the lives of the communities; in particular, with regard to the demands of the Jewish tradition for circumcision, acceptance of the purity codes, and other regulations of Jewish law contained in the Torah.

Our imagination of Paul's call on the Damascus road has been influenced by many paintings that so often include horses, such as the dramatic one by Caravaggio. It is interesting to note that neither Luke nor Paul make any such mention! Luke will relate the event on a number of occasions in Acts of the Apostles (Acts 9:1–22; 22:3–21; 26:1–20) and, while it is clear that these are written with a view to legitimating Paul and his mission, they are second hand accounts. In his own letters, Paul is somewhat circumspect and measured when he describes in Gal 1:16 how 'God revealed his Son to me' and gave him the mission to go to the Gentiles. He does claim this moment as one that legitimated him as an apostle and refers to it indirectly in 1 Cor 9:1, 'have I not seen the Lord?', and in 1 Cor 15:8, 'last of all, as to one untimely born, he appeared also to me.' In 2 Cor 12:2–4, Paul speaks in a thinly veiled way about his own experience, as one who was taken up into paradise and heard things that cannot be told. He speaks of this happening some fourteen years earlier. It's possible that this is the experience on the Damascus road.

Whatever else may be said, Paul's encounter with the Risen Lord radically changed the direction of his life from persecutor of the early Church to one of its strongest supporters. While it is natural to focus on that single event, there are other formative elements on Paul's journey of faith that are worth considering. One can only speculate, but what was the effect of conversations with Christians he had encountered in his zealous efforts to eradicate the **Nazarene heresy**? We will never know how much of his later belief was shaped by these encounters with Christians whose testimony and faithfulness were already preparing the soil for his later proclamation of Jesus as Messiah. Perhaps even more tantalising to ponder is the impact of his relatives Junia and Andronicus becoming Christians before him. (Rom 16:7)

Whether we can describe Paul going through a conversion from one faith to another will continue to be debated, but one thing that is absolutely certain is that he went through a process of assessment, and reconfiguring the way in which he saw the relationship of obedience to the Jewish law (Torah) and salvation. At least as far as Gentiles were concerned, the need for circumcision and faithfulness to all the requirements of the Torah was not to be demanded of Gentile Christians. Paul was convinced that it was to Gentiles in particular that he was given a mission to preach the Good News of Jesus Christ. It was his understanding of a mission to Gentiles with minimal adherence to the demands of the Torah that was to bring him into conflict with those Christians who shared his vision of Jesus' message being for all humanity, but disagreed as to the status of the Torah and to what degree Gentile Christians would need to follow its laws.

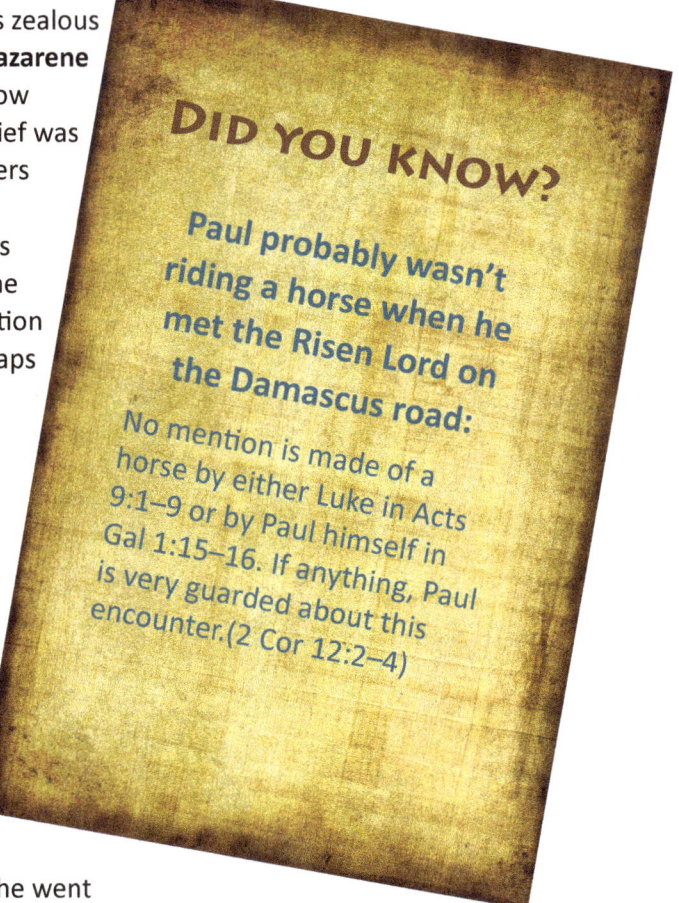

DID YOU KNOW?

Paul probably wasn't riding a horse when he met the Risen Lord on the Damascus road:

No mention is made of a horse by either Luke in Acts 9:1–9 or by Paul himself in Gal 1:15–16. If anything, Paul is very guarded about this encounter.(2 Cor 12:2–4)

Physical Description of Paul

Paul gives us no description of himself, and we should expect none given that the recipients of the letters, other the one addressed to the community in Rome, knew Paul well. In 2 Cor 10:10 he is well aware of the claims of his detractors that 'His letters are weighty and strong, but his bodily presence is weak, and his speech of no account.'

In the Syriac text of the *Acts of Paul and Thecla,* he is described as 'a man of middling size, and his hair was scanty, and his legs were a little crooked, and his knees were projecting, and he had large eyes and his eyebrows met, and his nose was somewhat long, and he was full of grace and mercy; at one time he seemed like a man, and at another time he seemed like an angel.'

This tends to bear out the fact that Paul's physical presence was such that he would not have fitted into any Greco-Roman models of attractiveness, or someone who had been blessed by the gods. In Gal 4:13–14 he admits that it was due to a physical infirmity that he first preached the Gospel message to the Galatians. Though he admits they would have been justified in treating him with scorn, the reverse was true; they treated him as a messenger sent from God.

This might indicate that his appearance belied his claims to be an apostle and servant of the living God. We also have to consider the mysterious reference to the 'thorn in the flesh' in 2 Cor 12:7. This has been variously explained as epilepsy, malaria, a disfigurement, or some other kind of disease. Given Paul's own description of imprisonments, shipwrecks, beatings and other dangers that he endured for the sake of the Gospel in 2 Cor 11:24–27, it is possible that these had left their mark on him physically. If that is true perhaps the description in the *Acts of Paul and Thecla* is more accurate than we might realize, as it speaks of Paul's spirit and character transcending appearances! There must have been something about him that could lead to the gathering of companions, and the founding of communities from Jerusalem to Illyricum.(Rom 15:19)

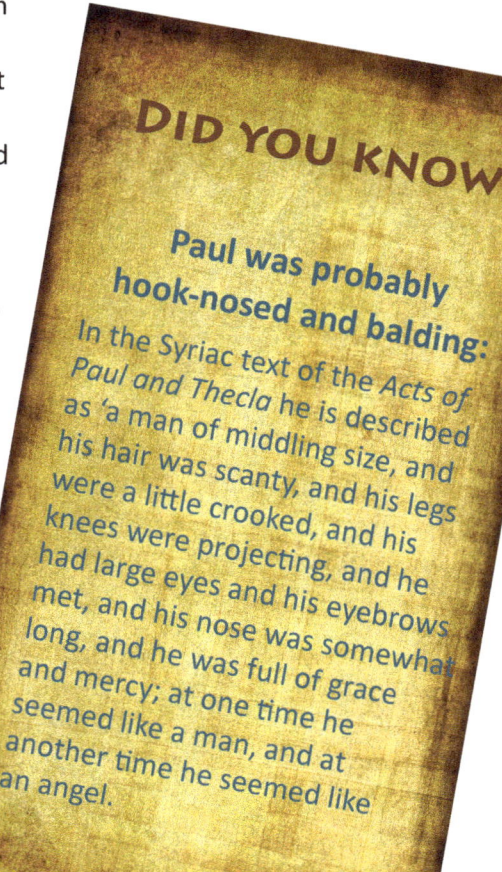

Did You Know?

Paul was probably hook-nosed and balding:
In the Syriac text of the *Acts of Paul and Thecla* he is described as 'a man of middling size, and his hair was scanty, and his legs were a little crooked, and his knees were projecting, and he had large eyes and his eyebrows met, and his nose was somewhat long, and he was full of grace and mercy; at one time he seemed like a man, and at another time he seemed like an angel.

Icon of Paul the Apostle

The *Acts of Paul and Thecla*

This is an apocryphal story (which means that it was not included in the Bible) written sometime prior to 190 CE, about a young woman, Thecla, who was inspired by Paul's teachings.

How Many Letters did Paul Write?

For the most part, the letters were not hand-written by Paul but dictated. In Gal 6:11 he notes *'See with what large letters I am writing to you with my own hand.'* There were good reasons for this since a scribe's writing was smaller and much more cost effective given the price of writing materials. In Rom 16:22 the Christian scribe Tertius adds his own greeting at the conclusion of the letter. Exceptions often prove the rule and the shortest of the letters addressed to Philemon is one that he claims to have written in his own hand (Phlm 19). One can imagine him engrossed in arguing one position or another, pacing up and down trying to articulate why his opponents were so patently wrong, or why his fledgling Christians in Corinth could still only be called babes in Christ ... while the scribe struggled to keep up!(cf. 1 Cor 3:1)

In the New Testament there are thirteen letters attributed to Paul. This testifies eloquently to how significant a figure he quickly became in the early growth and development of the Christian movement. It is likely that there are many more letters written by Paul than were preserved. 1 Cor 5:9 refers to advice given in an earlier letter, and 2 Cor 2:4 and 7:12 speak of the contentious letter Paul wrote after 1 Corinthians that is now lost to us.

Of the letters that are attributed to him, there are seven that are universally agreed to have been Paul's work: 1 Thessalonians, 1 Corinthians, 2 Corinthians, Romans, Galatians, Philippians, and the letter to Philemon.

Valentin de Boulogne (Circa 1600): Saint Paul writing his Epistles

So, what criteria are used to determine if Paul was the author of a letter? And what is the status of those letters not generally considered to have been written by Paul?

All the letters have been included in the New Testament, which attests to their ongoing value as inspired and valued texts. To say that Ephesians, Colossians, 1 and 2 Timothy, Titus, 2 Thessalonians and Hebrews are disputed as coming directly from Paul's hand does not mean they were not influenced by Paul, or that they did not come from those influenced by Paul who wanted to preserve his vision, or the ongoing development of his tradition. As has been observed from time to time, it is hard to know with precision where Paul ends and his legacy begins. The grounds on which these judgements are based come down to testing whether the vocabulary, organizational structures, or theology would fit into what we know of the Church during the period of Paul's ministry. Admittedly, this is an inexact science and debates about Ephesians, Colossians, and 2 Thessalonians will continue, as scholars continue to test the criteria that have been used to determine what is considered to have come from the hand of Paul.

There are strong indicators that ideas that were first expressed in Paul's undisputed letters come to be further developed within the circle of those communities influenced by him. The fact that letters were attributed to him was not an unusual occurrence in the ancient world, and it provides ample proof of the esteem in which he was held, and his ongoing influence within the early church.

Household Churches

In our world, where there are basilicas like St Peter's in Rome, Notre Dame in Paris, and countless cathedrals and churches built over centuries, it's perhaps difficult to imagine what it was like in the first decades of the Christian movement. They had no buildings in which to gather, and they were not even considered a religion at all, but a potentially dangerous superstition from the Roman province of Syria. As far as having places to gather there were limited possibilities: eating places of various kinds, shared spaces in apartment buildings (workshops or the like), or the households of rich patrons. The Pauline communities relied on the generosity of those community members who had their own households. Given from what we know of the size of these households, it would seem that communities might have been somewhere up to fifty to sixty people. It emerges from letters, such as those written to the Corinthians, that they gathered in a number of households.(cf. Rom 16:5; 1 Cor

11:22,34; 14:15; 16:15; Phil 4:22)

The Greco-Roman household was a much more complex and dynamic structure than our twenty-first century homes. Such households were not like the nuclear families of our own made up of parents and their children. They were more like an extended family, one that included slaves, co-workers, free men and women. In such households the head of the family (*pater familias*) held sway. It was clearly a patriarchal and hierarchical structure, and it was felt that order in the household was a microcosm of the empire at large. If the household functioned in an orderly fashion, so too did the city and, ultimately, the Empire itself.

The Pauline and **Deutero-Pauline** letters at times makes use of what are known as household codes, a familiar form of instruction regarding the good ordering of a household.(Col 3:18–4:1; Eph 5:22–33; 1 Tim 2:1–15) These instructions about husbands

left: An ancient Roman house

below: Floor plan of a household church

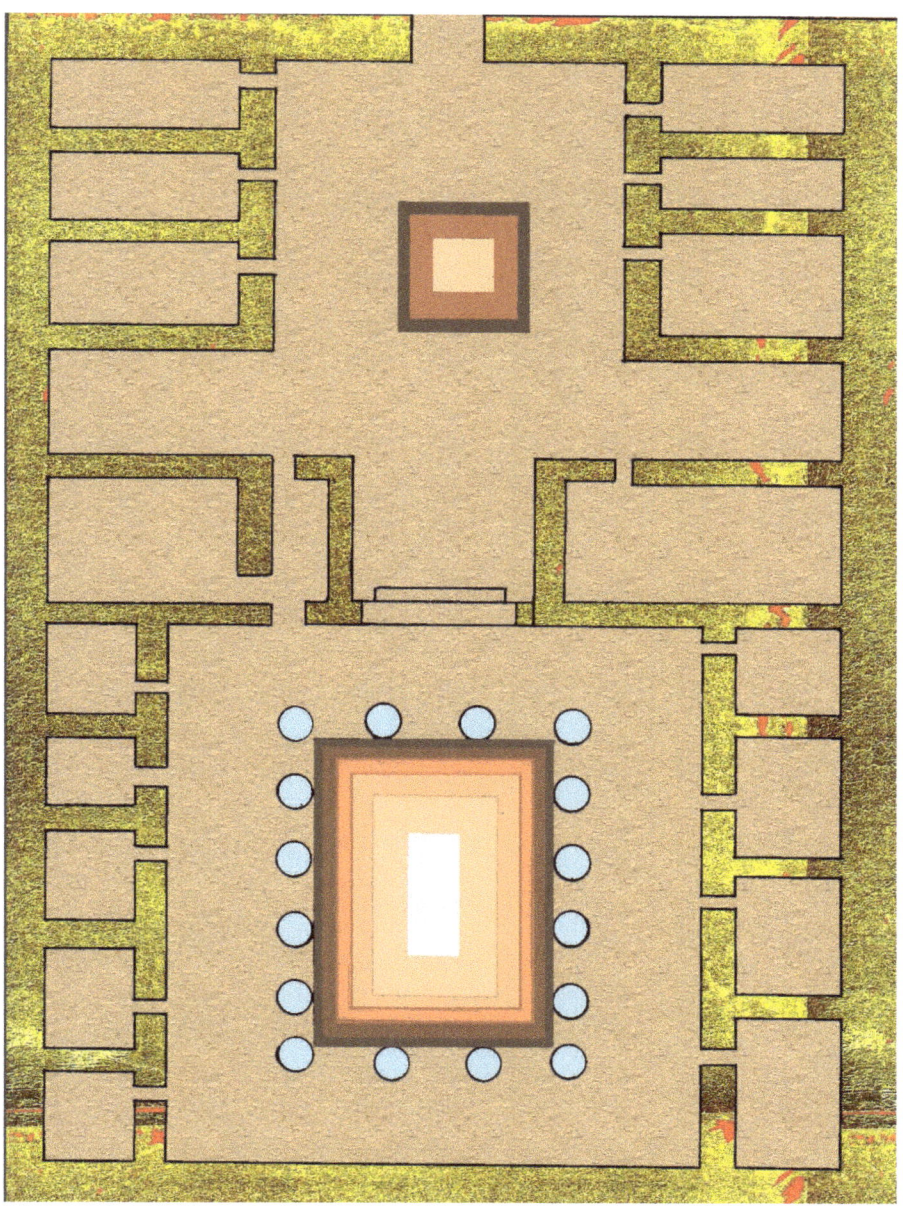

19

Deutero-Pauline

The term Deutero-Pauline may seem confusing and disconcerting at first because it leads the modern reader to confront the issue of whether all the letters attributed to Paul were written by him. For some time now it has been accepted that some of the Pauline letters in the New Testament were written by others—usually those who were followers of Paul—or those deeply influenced by his teaching. It was common practice in antiquity to attribute a later writing to a famous or honored person. Letters such as 1 and 2 Timothy and Titus witness to the development of the Pauline tradition, and the desire to honor his memory. For this reason they are called Deutero-Pauline, that is, a second stage of the Pauline tradition.

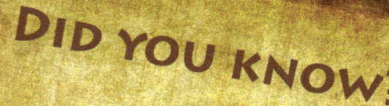

DID YOU KNOW?

Paul's communities gathered in homes (Rom 16:3–5):

'Greet Prisca and Aquila, who work with me in Christ Jesus, and who risked their necks for my life, to whom not only I give thanks, but also all the churches of the Gentiles. Greet also the church in their house.'

and wives, parents and children, masters and slaves made use of a well-established literary form and are culturally conditioned. There is no doubt that some of this material is problematic viewed from a twenty-first century perspective. It inevitably raises the question as to how such texts are to be used in our own context where the starting point is one of equality and co-responsibility, and where slavery should have no place. It is both natural and necessary that these texts be tested and it is instructive to note that even from the beginnings of Christianity there were tensions with the existing patterns for the ordering of society. In Gal 3:28, the vision of a new humanity is outlined where there is no longer slave or free, woman or man, Jew or Greek. But how were Christians going to order their lives and manage their households? It must have been very difficult to establish new ways of thinking and acting that were consistent with their baptism into the death and resurrection of Jesus.

It is fascinating to explore questions of how these communities were organized, and who exercised spiritual authority. If the leader of the household became a Christian the rest of the household would have followed e.g. Lydia.(Acts 16:15) Within a polytheistic religious context this was perhaps not such a problem, but how many of the slaves and freed men and women really decided to become Christians at all, at least as far as we would understand it? This may partly explain some of the chaos that accompanied the Eucharistic celebrations in Corinth where the rich were well fed and drunk before the slaves and others had finished their duties and were able to attend.(1 Cor 11:21–22)

In a world that was highly structured along the lines of honour and shame, the building of Christian communities as an example of a new humanity would have been very difficult indeed. Dining rooms had limited capacity and places at a table were determined on the basis of power and prestige.(cf. Jesus' instructions on this matter in Luke 14:7–13) Paul was offended by the lack of dignity afforded to the poor among the community and reminded the Corinthians in 1 Cor 8:11 that they were all brothers and sisters 'for whom Christ died.'

Who would have led the Eucharistic celebrations? And who had spiritual authority? What happened if the person was a slave, a deacon like Chloe, or someone who was normally seen as an inferior? It was one thing to speak of being a new humanity made up of slaves and free, women and men, but it was another thing entirely to begin the process of becoming that new humanity and dealing with the practical consequences of such a belief. The annual pagan festival of Saturnalia enabled slaves and masters to change roles for a short time, but no one saw this as a model for a new society. The brutal suppression of the slave revolt of Spartacus in 73–71 BCE shows how dependent Rome was on slavery, and the measures that would be taken to ensure its continuance.

Paul and his Co-workers

While it is natural that we focus our attention on Paul, the letters make obvious that he did not work in isolation, but in conjunction with many others in a quickly developing network that extended across the newly formed communities. In the letters, references are made to co-workers as brothers and sisters, like Phoebe and Sosthenes (Rom 16:1; 1 Cor 1:1), or as apostles such as Junia and Silas.(Rom 16:7; 1 Thess 2:7) Timothy is called at different times a brother (2 Cor 1:1), apostle (1 Thess 2:7), fellow slave (Phil 1:1) and co-worker. (Rom 16:21)

Paul worked with husband and wife teams such as Aquila and Prisca in Corinth and Asia Minor (Rom 16:3–5), and had a loose, and perhaps tense relationship at times with Apollos in Corinth and elsewhere.(1 Cor 3:5,9; 4:9; 16:12) His long working relationship with Barnabas is clear in 1 Cor 9:6, and in Gal 2:1,9,13. Co-workers such as Titus carried Paul's severe letter to Corinth, indicating that not only did Paul trust in his ability to convey his message, but that Titus had the capacity to build bridges that were very much in danger of being knocked down by mistrust and misunderstanding. (2 Cor 2:13; 8:16–23) Delegates such as Titus were sent into the lions' den when Paul was in conflict with various points of view and individuals in a community, and they were the ones entrusted with the duty of convincing the communities to reassess their positions in the light of Paul's advice.

People such as Sosthenes (1 Cor 1:1) and Timothy (2 Cor 1:1; Philemon 1) are mentioned at the beginning of letters as co-senders and were clearly expected to be known and respected by the recipients of the letters. The conclusions of some of the letters are helpful in providing the names of co-workers who were traveling from one city to another. In Rom 16:1–2, Phoebe, the deacon of Corinth traveling to Rome, is named as worthy of support and her kindness as a benefactor to Paul and others noted. In 1 Cor 16:10, Timothy is recommended so that when he arrives in Corinth he will be afforded the welcome and support that Paul considers appropriate for a trusted co-worker.

In each of the communities that Paul established, patterns of leadership needed to be developed and leaders appointed in order for the communities to continue to grow after Paul moved on to establish other communities. 1 Cor 15:16–17 urges the community to give support to people such as Stephanus, Fortunatus and Achaicus who were clearly leaders in the community.

An important group of Pauline co-workers were those wealthy Christians who made their households available as meeting places for worship and other Christian gatherings. As mentioned previously, their generosity was something that needed to be treated very carefully, since it ran the culturally conditioned risk of establishing patterns of indebtedness in terms of dealing with others as clients or patrons, patterns that would undermine the formation and development of vibrant Christian communities.

21

Getting a Handle on Paul's Thought: Some Key Pauline concepts

Given that the letters were written to particular communities addressing quite specific questions, it would be too much to expect that we can accurately reconstruct all of the richness and complexity of Paul's thought. This is not to say that there are not recurring themes, or that letters such as Romans do not go a long way towards providing some major indications as to the scope and depth of Paul's theology, his understanding of the death and resurrection of Jesus, or the life of the Church. It is more a caution along the lines of not presuming that all that Paul's communities, and his circle of co-workers, thought and believed is captured in the letters. In the end this is not so different from acknowledging that a few photos taken from a photo album will say all that can be said of a person's life and experience. In a similar way the letters are snapshots of the life and belief of the first generations of Christians. It was a dynamic period when the foundations were being laid, when the very language that we consider to be typically Christian was being developed.

These letters represent the first attempts to articulate their beliefs in written form decades before the Gospels were written. A consequence of this is that we should not expect them to have every concept or theme clearly or systematically formulated: that has come after centuries of reflection, study and debate that built on their foundation. Modern readers of these letters are often surprised to find that events in the life of Jesus and his sayings that are so familiar to us from the Gospels are not mentioned in the letters of Paul. An exception is the tradition that Paul had received information about the last supper in 1 Cor 11:23–26. In this instance, and in 1 Cor 15:3–4, dealing with the bodily resurrection of both Jesus and those who follow him, Paul explicitly refers to the tradition that he had received from others. In Gal 1:18 Paul makes mention of his first trip to Jerusalem to visit Peter for two weeks, and Gal 2:1 refers to a visit some fourteen years later when he was given the mandate to preach the Gospel to the Gentiles. These moments, and others when his path intersected with various apostles and evangelists on the road, would have provided opportunities to share the traditions of Jesus with other leaders within the communities. This is a roundabout way of saying that just because Paul does not refer to the sayings of Jesus, it does not mean that he, and the communities that he established and served, were not aware of them.

One of the things that is distinctive about Paul is that he talks not so much about what Jesus said and did, as much as focus on the meaning of Jesus' life, death and resurrection. In the letters, we witness Paul unpacking for his converts and readers the consequences of the life of Jesus as he struggles to articulate how the crucified and Risen one is the Lord, and how this one life that appeared to end in abject failure has the power to literally change everything God has created. Paul is a big picture person and the big picture is one in which God is faithful to promises made to Israel and all creation. Scholars continue to debate whether there is a key idea or theme in his thought, or whether the answer lies more in the narrative that underlies the many themes and images found within the letters.

Time is short and Jesus is at the heart of it

Paul's framework for understanding the life, death and resurrection of Jesus is the expectation of Second Temple Judaism, for a Messiah who would usher in the age to come. The Messiah's coming would set to right injustices, and the powerlessness of the Jewish people *in the present time* would finally come to an end. Understandably, many of Paul's contemporaries longed for this promised Day of the Lord. It would be a time when their faithfulness to the demands of the Covenant would be vindicated, wounds healed, and justice established. God's longed for reign would finally begin, not only for Israel, but for all people. While Paul does not speak of the Kingdom of God with the same frequency as is found in Jesus' teachings and parables in the Gospels, it is, nonetheless, a theme that is present in the letters.(cf. Rom 14:17; 1 Cor 15:24; Col 1:13)

⁵ Let the same mind be in you that was in Christ Jesus, ⁶ who, though he was in the form of God, did not regard equality with God as something to be exploited, ⁷ but emptied himself, taking the form of a slave, being born in human likeness. And being found in human form, ⁸ he humbled himself and became obedient to the point of death—even death on a cross. ⁹ Therefore God also highly exalted him and gave him the name that is above every name, ¹⁰ so that at the name of Jesus every knee should bend, in heaven and on earth and under the earth, ¹¹ and every tongue should confess that Jesus Christ is Lord, to the glory of God the Father.

PHILIPPIANS 2:5–11

above: Crucifixion fresco, San Marco church, Milan

Paul saw the dawning of that age was ushered in by the death and resurrection of Jesus. Now a new age had dawned, though it was not yet fully inaugurated, and Christians awaited Jesus' return at the end of time, when Jesus would hand back all of creation to God having conquered sin, and even death itself. In 1 Cor 15:24 he describes it as: 'Then comes the end, when he hands over the kingdom to God the Father, after he has destroyed every ruler and every authority and power.'

In Gal 4:4, the birth of Jesus is spoken of as coming at 'the fullness of time', indicating how this birth was understood to play a critical role in the unfolding of God's saving history for the world. This present time Paul refers to in Gal 1:4 as an 'evil age.' This sort of terminology indicates the sense of struggle and turmoil that these early Christians experienced. In Phil 2:15, Paul exhorts the community to use the present moment as a time to witness to their faith by the quality of their lives, to 'shine like stars in the world', a world judged to be perverse and crooked. The letters attest to the understanding of this present time as one where the ruler of this world continues to battle against Christians.

While the new age had been inaugurated, it will not come in its fullness until the return of Jesus at the end of time. Until that moment, Paul and his Christians live in a world where sin and death continue to be realities. It is in this context that Paul interprets opposition encountered as being the direct work of Satan. In 1 Thess 2:18, his inability to return to Thessalonica was seen to be the direct consequence of the opposition provided by Satan: 'For we wanted to come to you—certainly I, Paul, wanted to again and again—but Satan blocked our way.' Even the opposition provided by other Christians could at times be interpreted as due to the efforts of Satan. In 2 Cor 2:11 he urges the community to forgive the one who opposed him. He explains: 'And we do this so that we may not be outwitted by Satan; for we are not ignorant of his designs.'

> I mean, brothers and sisters, the appointed time has grown short; from now on, let even those who have wives be as though they had none…
> 1 CORINTHIANS 7:29

It is in this context too that one can appreciate Paul's reference to powers, authorities and dominions. While Christians continued to live in the world, the old age remained, and it was not giving up without a fight. In 1 Cor 15:28, Paul looked forward to the day of Christ's final victory, 'When all things are subjected to him, then the Son himself will also be subjected to the one who put all things in subjection under him, so that God may be all in all.'

Paul and his communities expected that the Lord's return would come soon, and the letters attest to this in a number of ways. There are repeated references to the Day of the Lord. In 1 Thess 5:2 it is described as coming upon us like a thief in the night.(cf. 1 Thess 5:4; 1 Cor 5:5; 2 Cor 1:14) There are also texts that witness to the belief that many of Paul's community would still be alive when the Lord returned. A well-known example of this is 1 Thess 4:14–17 where the Christians of Thessalonica are comforted concerning those Christians who have already died. In this passage he makes clear what his own understanding is of the sequence of events at the end of time. Those Christians who have died will be raised: 'Then we who are alive, who are left, will be caught up in the clouds together with them to meet the Lord in the air; and so we will be with the Lord forever.' (1 Thess 4:17)

Paul's belief that time was short gives an intensity and urgency to his instructions to his communities that has naturally been dulled over nearly two millennia of Christian living. Keeping this view of time in mind is particularly helpful when reading his advice on marriage and slavery in 1 Cor 7, otherwise he can be wrongly understood to be condoning slavery and devaluing marriage. In Corinth the situation was that some Christians believed that they should split up existing marriages and stop newly engaged couples from getting married so that they could prepare for the Lord's coming, as they saw it, in an appropriately focused manner. Having been asked for his advice on the matter it seems that Paul had some sympathy with their position. He couches his advice carefully saying that 'I think that, in view of the impending crisis, it is well for you to remain as you are.'(1 Cor 7:26)

By this he means that—in the light of the imminent changes and suffering that would accompany Jesus' return—slaves, married, and betrothed should not seek to

change their state, but prepare for the Day of the Lord. It is critical that we understood the context from which Paul is writing in order to be able to interpret these texts correctly, and only then apply them to our own context. His advice was based on a certain understanding of time. It is not unreasonable to suppose that if his advice on marriage was requested today it would be quite different considering that, after nearly two thousand years, Jesus is yet to return.

Paul and Judaism

One of the intensely debated areas in Pauline studies has been that of determining Paul's relationship to Judaism, with its focus on where Paul stands with regard to his own tradition. Does he stand within his tradition or outside it? That there is a debate indicates that there is material from the letters of Paul that can be used to argue for either side. There are texts that are negative concerning Jewish practices, such as in Phil 3:2, where Paul talks about circumcision as mutilation, or in 2 Cor 3:7, where he speaks of the old covenant as a ministry of death carved on stone. On the other hand, Paul's teaching contains quotations from the scriptures, and there are over one hundred explicit citations of Old Testament passages, not to mention many other allusions.

It is here that the caution mentioned earlier concerning looking at each letter in its own context comes into its own. A case in point would be the letter to the Galatians: written for a group of Gentile Christians who are being encouraged by Jewish Christians to be circumcised and follow some of the demands of the Jewish law. It is a letter in which Paul defends his own approach in which circumcision is not demanded for Gentiles who become Christians. Paul warns the Galatians that anyone who teaches another form of the Gospel message than the one he taught should be handed over for destruction (a polite way of saying they could go to hell). One would not be surprised to learn that such a sentiment has been used to argue that Paul no longer valued or adhered to the demands of his own Jewish tradition.

Here it is important to weigh matters carefully, particularly in light of the rhetorical purpose of this letter, that is, to get the Galatians to remain faithful to the form of Christianity to which they had been introduced by Paul. It is less a matter of Paul arguing against his own tradition, and more a matter of ensuring that the Galatians not accept unnecessary burdens in order to continue to be members of the Christian community. It is true that in Phil 3:8 Paul says that he regards everything of his former life in Judaism as so much rubbish if only he can know Christ. Compared to Christ, everything else pales. However, this is not to say that his tradition was no longer precious or valued. In Rom 9:1–5 Paul expresses powerfully his love and appreciation of the Jewish tradition and its privileged status: 'They are Israelites, and to them belong the adoption, the glory, the covenants, the giving of the law, the worship, and the promises; to them belong the patriarchs, and from them, according to the flesh, comes the Messiah, who is over all, God blessed forever. Amen.'

⁸ More than that, I regard everything as loss because of the surpassing value of knowing Christ Jesus my Lord. For his sake I have suffered the loss of all things, and I regard them as rubbish, in order that I may gain Christ.
Phil 3:8

¹I am speaking the truth in Christ—I am not lying; my conscience confirms it by the Holy Spirit— ² I have great sorrow and unceasing anguish in my heart. ³ For I could wish that I myself were accursed and cut off from Christ for the sake of my own people, my kindred according to the flesh. ⁴ They are Israelites, and to them belong the adoption, the glory, the covenants, the giving of the law, the worship, and the promises; ⁵ to them belong the patriarchs, and from them, according to the flesh, comes the Messiah, who is over all, God blessed forever. Amen.
Rom 9:1–5

The letters reveal time and time again that Paul continued to draw on the scriptures as a compass for right behaviour, and as a source for his teaching. He was, and continued to be, deeply steeped in his tradition. Where he parted company with other Jewish Christians was in his judgement of what should be required of Gentile Christians. These were highly emotive and sensitive matters and needed to be addressed so that Jewish and Gentile Christians were able to celebrate the Eucharist together. One only needs to look to Gal 2:11–14 where Paul refers to his public condemnation of Peter for his inconsistency in this matter. Formerly, Peter had engaged in table fellowship with Gentile Christians but, when members of the community came from Jerusalem, he changed his attitude and his evangelical practice.

[11] But when Cëphas came to Antioch, I opposed him to his face, because he stood self-condemned; [12] for until certain people came from James, he used to eat with the Gentiles. But after they came, he drew back and kept himself separate for fear of the circumcision faction. [13] And the other Jews joined him in this hypocrisy, so that even Barnabas was led astray by their hypocrisy. [14] But when I saw that they were not acting consistently with the truth of the gospel, I said to Cëphas before them all, "If you, though a Jew, live like a Gentile and not like a Jew, how can you compel the Gentiles to live like Jews?"
GAL 2:11–14

> **DID YOU KNOW?**
> Paul had relatives who were Christians before him (Rom 16:7):
> 'Greet Andronicus and Junia, my relatives who were in prison with me; they are prominent among the apostles, and they were in Christ before I was.'

For Paul this was too much and he publically challenged Peter about his behaviour. From Paul's perspective, the covenant with Moses had an important educational and custodial role to play until the coming of the Messiah.(Gal 3:24) Paul's co-religionists argued that the law had been given to Moses by God, and it was not to be changed under any circumstances. His response in Gal 3:17–18 is to remind them that there was an earlier covenant made with Abraham that had not been repealed. After the coming of the Messiah it was now coming to its fulfilment, in particular, by means of the inclusion of the Gentiles.

Paul knew the scriptures well and uses the covenant with Abraham for two reasons. The first is that Gal 3:6 refers to Gen 15:6, where Abraham was declared to be righteous before God before the requirement for circumcision was brought into effect, thereby showing that circumcision isn't needed to be in right relationship with God. The second reason is that God in Gen 12:3 had promised Abraham that all the nations would be blessed through him, thereby bringing them into God's saving plan, and this text is used by Paul in Gal 3:8. The model of Abraham clearly became an important part of Paul's understanding and justification for his mission, because what he developed in the letter to the Galatians is then picked up and further developed in Rom 4.

In 1 Cor 9:20–21, Paul makes the interesting remark that he is a Jew with Jews, and a Gentile with Gentiles, in order that he might by all means save people for Christ. This gives a glimpse into his missionary strategy, which would have been one sensitive to the particular audience—be it Jewish or Gentile—to whom he addressed his message. The more polemical passages in the letters have a context where communities that Paul and his co-workers have established were ones where many Jewish practices were not required of them in order to be Christian, and have now been visited by Jewish Christians who are questioning Paul's minimal requirements. One suspects that they were saying that Paul had done well in establishing the community, but if a person really wanted to complete the process of becoming a Christian, then adherence to the law and circumcision was required. In the face of such teaching, Paul reacted strongly and the modern reader needs to be careful in distinguishing between what is said in the midst of a heated debate, and what Paul would have said when asked about the beauty and richness of his tradition that continued to shape his understanding of Jesus and Christianity till the day he died.

[20] Where is the one who is wise? Where is the scribe? Where is the debater of this age? Has not God made foolish the wisdom of the world? [21] For since, in the wisdom of God, the world did not know God through wisdom, God decided, through the foolishness of our proclamation, to save those who believe.
1 COR 9:20–21

THE DEATH OF JESUS

The death and resurrection of Jesus is the foundational event that Paul refers to time and time again. Much of the language we generally consider to be distinctively Christian—words such as salvation, redemption and atonement—originally came to be used in response to the questions that naturally arose in the process of preaching the message in various contexts. Paul turned to a wide range of images and language to answer a fundamental question, namely: what difference does the death and resurrection of Jesus make to us and the world?

When he speaks of the death of

Jesus as foolishness to Greeks and a stumbling block to Jews in 1 Cor 1:22–24, it is based on his sometimes bitter experience of teaching, and countless beatings and imprisonments suffered for the sake of the Gospel. The message of the Galilean carpenter who was killed and now claimed to be raised from the dead was an exceedingly challenging message to preach. Yet this remained the core of Paul's Gospel and the letters attest to the variety of ways he articulated for his fledgling communities the importance of the paschal mystery for all people and all times. It is in unpacking the consequences of the death and resurrection of Jesus that Paul was at his most creative.

[22] For Jews demand signs and Greeks desire wisdom, [23] but we proclaim Christ crucified, a stumbling block to Jews and foolishness to Gentiles, [24] but to those who are the called, both Jews and Greeks, Christ the power of God and the wisdom of God.
1 Cor 1:22–24

One of Paul's great contributions to the development of Christian thought is that of the many ways in which the consequences of the death of Jesus are expressed in his letters. This brutal death is first of all seen through the filter of God's faithful love to humanity and all of creation. A new beginning is now possible. Adam, through whom sin and death came into the world, is compared to Jesus who—as the new Adam—brings life.(Rom 5:12–21; 1 Cor 15:20–22) The death and resurrection of Jesus ushers in a new age and Paul speaks of this as a new creation.(2 Cor 5:17; Gal 6:15) Much of the rich tapestry of images used by Paul have a relational focus and speak of reconciliation (Rom 5:11; 2 Cor 5:18–19), or justification (Rom 4:24; 5:18; Gal 2:21)—that is, being in right relationship with God and others. The sacrificial language of atonement (Rom 3:25), so foreign to people of today, is also used to express the belief that just as the sacrifice of animals in the Jewish Temple, and in the Temples of Greco-Roman religions, maintained or healed our relationship with God, so too, Jesus' death brought humanity into right relationship with God. Paul also uses the language of redemption (Rom 3:24; 8:23; 1 Cor 1:30)—that is, the buying back of slaves—to speak of the death of Jesus.

In other contexts, the language of salvation (1 Thess 5:8–9; Rom 1:16; 11:11; 13:11; 2 Cor 6:2)—that is, of rescuing someone—is used to capture something of the beauty of what has been achieved in the death of Jesus. To this day people ask the question: why did Jesus die? And why is it that a loving God makes the death of Jesus an atonement for human sin? These are profound questions and some of the Pauline language can give the impression of a vengeful and angry God demanding blood to heal the wounds caused by sin. In order to appreciate what Paul means when he speaks of the wrath of God (Rom 1:18; 5:9), it needs to be recognised that he does not refer so much to the feeling of anger on God's part, as much as a commitment to eliminate what does not properly belong in God's creative plan—that is: sin. This commitment is shown on God's part by sending Jesus to heal what humanity could not. In Rom 1–3, Paul outlines the plight of humanity that had lost its way, be it Jews or Gentiles: 'all have sinned and fall short of the glory of God.'(Rom 3:23) But all is far from lost because 'God proves his love for us in that while we still were sinners Christ died for us.'(Rom 5:8)

In other words God does for us what we cannot do for ourselves.

Jesus' death becomes an example and model for all Christian living. The beautiful hymn from Phil 2:5–11 articulates the profound belief that Jesus' humble outpouring of his life in service and love, even unto death, is the model for all Christian living. Everything is to be based on this extraordinary gift of love. As Paul puts it succinctly: 'And the life I now live in the flesh I live by faith in the Son of God, who loved me and gave himself for me.'(Gal 2:20)

DID YOU KNOW?
Paul believed Jesus would return in his lifetime (1 Thess 4:16–17):

'For the Lord himself, with a cry of command, with the archangel's call and with the sound of God's trumpet, will descend from heaven, and the dead in Christ will rise first. Then we who are alive, who are left, will be caught up in the clouds together with them to meet the Lord in the air; and so we will be with the Lord forever.'

(1 Thess 4:16–17):
'For you yourselves know very well that the day of the Lord will come like a thief in the night.'

Paul and Community

Given that the death of Jesus enables the birth of a new humanity, reconciled to God and to one another, it should come as no surprise that the creation and maintaining of a Christian community is a major concern in Paul's letters. In Gal 3:28 mention is made that there is no longer slave nor free, woman or man, Jew or Greek. It is a radical view of a different world to the one in which the Pauline communities lived, where gender, religion and status determined both how a person judged themself, and how he or she was judged by others.

Most people were not what we would consider 'free', with limited possibilities to participate fully in the life of their city. It is instructive that the very word that Paul uses for church, *ekklesia*, is a word that resonated on a number of levels for his contemporaries. It was a word used to describe an assembly of a small group of free citizens who gathered to debate and consider the issues facing a city. As such it was a political word. It was also the same word that was used in the Greek translation of the Old Testament to describe the assembly of the people of God gathered for worship, or other purposes such as a holy war. In a world where most people had no vote, and were largely marginalized, the Pauline communities use a political and religious word to describe themselves.

We can only begin to imagine how powerful and exciting it was for them to consider that in their newly established community of believers, where everybody shared the same dignity by virtue of their baptism into the death and resurrection of Jesus, that a new humanity was being established. Slaves would now have a voice, and be able to call their masters brother or sister. By virtue of baptism, everybody had a dignity that needed to be honoured and respected. This would have run against the norms of Greco-Roman culture that was hierarchical, where relationships of patrons and clients were determined by duties and responsibilities, as well as the ongoing competition for honour.

One doesn't have to scratch too deeply in the letters to see that the transition into this new vision of humanity was not an easy one for many to accept or accommodate in the communities. Old patterns of being did not simply cease to exist after undergoing the ritual of baptism. The rich were still rich, and the poor were still poor; slaves were still expected to serve their masters. Something of the hope and frustration can be sensed in Rom 8:22–23 where Paul says:

> We know that the whole creation has been groaning in labour pains until now; and not only the creation, but we ourselves, who have the first fruits of the Spirit, groan inwardly while we wait for adoption, the redemption of our bodies.

The letters reveal that the creation of a new humanity was no easy matter, and they are shot through with demands to live as a new humanity, founded on love, where the fruits of the Spirit are manifested by the desire to compete only in terms of showing honour to others (Rom 12:10), where love provides the basis for actions rather than knowledge (1 Cor 8:1), where the other person is seen and respected as a brother and sister for whom Christ died (1 Cor 8:11), and where all actions are to be based on the example of Jesus' humble outpouring of his life and self for others.(Phil 2:5–11)

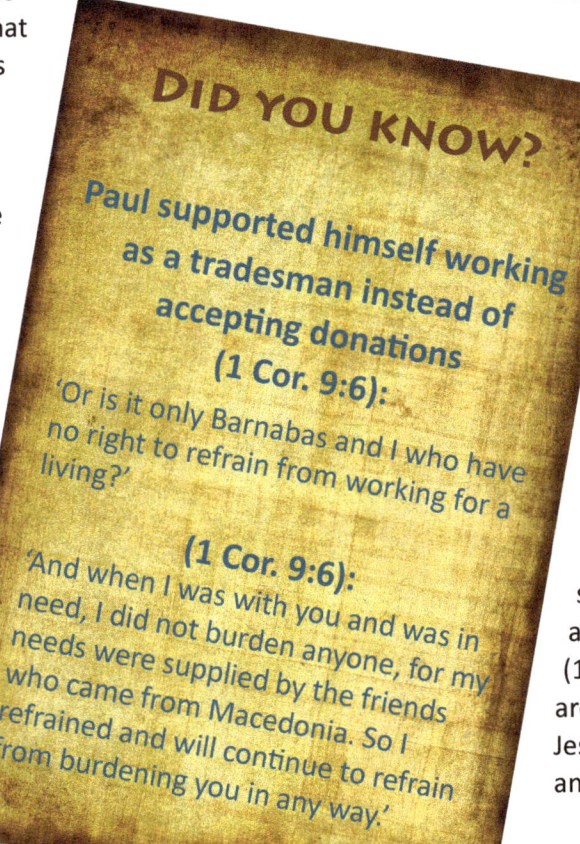

DID YOU KNOW?

Paul supported himself working as a tradesman instead of accepting donations

(1 Cor. 9:6):
'Or is it only Barnabas and I who have no right to refrain from working for a living?'

(1 Cor. 9:6):
'And when I was with you and was in need, I did not burden anyone, for my needs were supplied by the friends who came from Macedonia. So I refrained and will continue to refrain from burdening you in any way.'

The Importance of Women in the Pauline Communities

One of the most emotionally charged areas of the study of Paul is that of considering his attitude towards women. It is understandable from a twenty-first century perspective his calls for women to be silent in the religious assembly (1 Cor 14:34), or to wear veils (1 Cor 11:5), or be subject to their husbands (Eph 5:22) are not well received and support the view that he was patriarchal and authoritarian. It is true that Paul would have been conditioned, as we all are, by his cultural and religious context, and that this can be interpreted positively or negatively by subsequent generations.

In fairness to Paul, all of the evidence needs to be considered and evaluated before judging him as a misogynist. In 1 Cor 11, where Paul calls for women to wear veils in the assembly, he presumes that they are exercising spiritual leadership in the community as prophets, and this cannot be done by being silent in the assembly! One of the possible explanations for his call for them to wear veils is to avoid being mistaken for one of the mystery cults of the time, where women would let down their hair in a frenzy. This was interpreted as a sign of entering into some form of spiritual state. Unfortunately, Paul justifies his argument by reverting to hierarchical language that is singularly unhelpful in our modern context.

The text that comes later in the letter in 1 Cor 14:34, asking for the women to be silent in the assembly, is one that is notoriously difficult to pin down as to its precise meaning. It would have been clear to the Corinthians, and they would have had the advantage of being able to ask the bearer of the letter to explain Paul's advice on the matter. The context in 1 Cor 14 is that of dealing with disorderly conduct in communal worship, and a mixed community of Jews and Gentiles would have had a wide variety of expectations as to what would be acceptable in a worship situation, especially if it was in a household setting. The light that 1 Cor 11 sheds on the matter is that women could not exercise the ministry of prophecy and be silent. Whatever is intended by Paul in 1 Cor 14:34, it does not cancel out what he had previously indicated about women prophets 1 Cor 11.

The profile that can be built up from the letters is that while Paul can be rightly spoken of as being patriarchal, he nonetheless clearly recognized and supported the leadership of women. In Rom 16:1–2,

> **Did you know?**
> There were women deacons in Paul's time (Rom 16:1):
> 'I commend to you our sister Phoebe, a deacon of the church at Cenchreae.'

he recommends Phoebe, who was a deacon and leader in the Corinthian house church in Cenchreae, when she is travelling to Rome; and Rom 16:12 mentions two sisters: Tryphaena and Tryphosa, along with another woman called Persis, who are praised as co-workers. In Phil 4:2–3, Euodia and Syntyche are also identified as co-workers.

Aquila and Prisca worked with Paul as a husband and wife partnership of apostles, establishing household churches in Corinth, and Ephesus (Rom 16:3; 1 Cor 16:19), and Junia and Andronicus are also likewise singled out in their ministry in Rom 16:7. 1 Cor 9:5 provides a snapshot of the early Church where husbands and wives ministered alongside one another. 'Do we not have the right to be accompanied by a believing wife, as do the other apostles and the brothers of the Lord and Cephas?' Such texts serve to correct any tendency to jump to false conclusions that would limit the role played by women in the Pauline communities.

Within 1 Cor 7, Paul makes it very clear that both husbands and wives have mutual responsibilities and obligations. One partner could not make decisions about their marital responsibilities without the consent of the other. His advice is based on the principle that 'For the wife does not have authority over her own body, but the husband does; likewise the husband does not have authority over his own body, but the wife does.'(1 Cor. 7:4) Even in Eph 5 it is clear that, while women are called to be subject to their husbands, the husbands are similarly challenged. 'In the same way, husbands should love their wives as they do their own bodies. He who loves his wife loves himself.'(Eph 5:28) It is also interesting to note in Eph 5:21, before husbands and wives are addressed specifically, the whole community is called to: 'Be subject to one another out of reverence for Christ.'

One of Paul's leading ideas is that of a new creation (2 Cor 5:17, Gal 6:15) and one of the consequences of this new time in salvation history is that pre-existing and well-entrenched divisions are now being called into question since: 'There is no longer Jew or Greek, there is no longer slave or free, there is no longer male and female; for all of you are one in Christ Jesus.'(Gal 3:28)

The question as to whether Paul was married is an intriguing one, and it is not one that can be simply answered, or brushed aside too quickly. Some versions of 1 Cor 7:7 translate the verse as though Paul was single, but the matter is more nuanced than that. What he says in 1 Cor 7:7 is 'I wish that all were as I myself am. But each has a particular gift from God, one having one kind and another a different kind.' This could mean a number of things: he might be a widower, he might be single, or, if he is married, they are living separate from one another on account of Paul's mission; which is possible, given the dangers that he faced. In Phil 4:3 Paul asks his 'loyal companion' to intervene in a disagreement between Euodia and Syntyche, two leading women in the community. This word is usually used of a spouse, and it may indicate that, if married, his spouse lived in Philippi. It could explain his powerful bond with this particular community, and why it assisted Paul so consistently.

At the end of this snapshot of women in the Pauline communities, what can be said? It is clear that there are texts where Paul's advice reflects a patriarchal and hierarchical way of thinking. In fairness to Paul, there are other texts that go well beyond what we would expect in his religious and cultural context. He might have been patriarchal in dealing with some issues, but in the light of the evidence that indicates there were many women leaders in the Pauline communities, it would be unfair to brand him a misogynist.

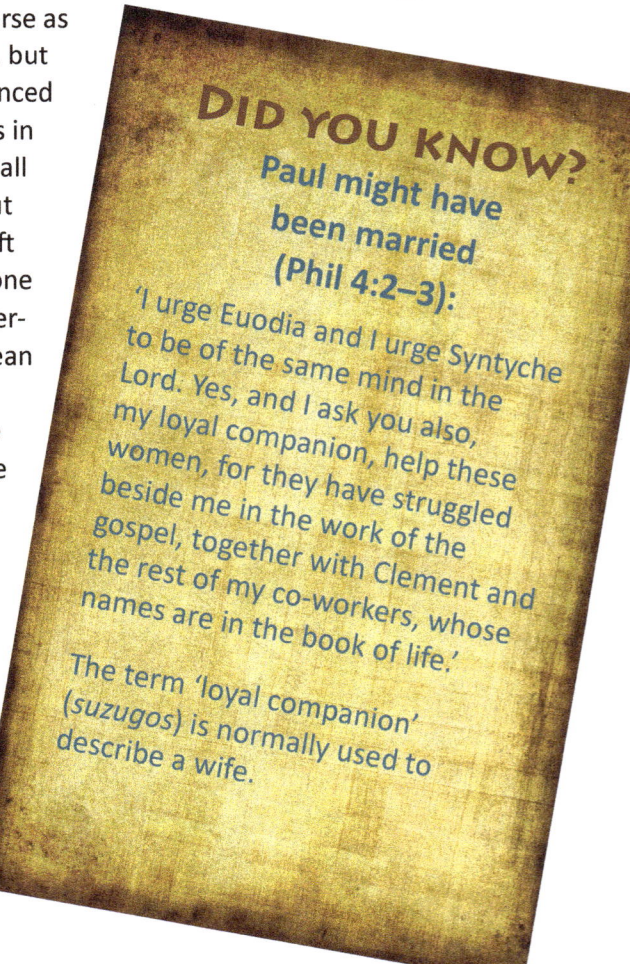

DID YOU KNOW?
Paul might have been married (Phil 4:2–3):

'I urge Euodia and I urge Syntyche to be of the same mind in the Lord. Yes, and I ask you also, my loyal companion, help these women, for they have struggled beside me in the work of the gospel, together with Clement and the rest of my co-workers, whose names are in the book of life.'

The term 'loyal companion' (*suzugos*) is normally used to describe a wife.

THE LETTERS OF PAUL

Latrine and Frontinus gate of Heirapolis, Turkey

1 Thessalonians

Possibly written from Corinth (Approx. 50–51 AD)

It is generally agreed that among the preserved letters of Paul, 1 Thessalonians is the first written. It is primarily a letter of friendship, support and encouragement. When Paul wrote to them, the Thessalonian Christians had already suffered much for the sake of the Gospel. (1 Thess 1:6) Paul had to preach the Gospel to them 'in the face of concern for them, he sent Timothy to support them in their trials. Timothy returned to Paul with an encouraging report of their steadfast faith.(cf. 1 Thess 3:7–8) At the time of writing the letter, Paul still hoped to visit the community in the near future.

Paul's advice in 1 Thess 4:1–8 on holiness and chastity points to some of the clear changes of point of view and behaviour that were required in order to become a Christian. It was one thing to become a part of the community, and another and it enabled him to move into a new city and support himself while establishing a community, ensuring his own independence, and thereby avoiding being treated as a client of a rich patron.

One of the elements of 1 Thessalonians that has drawn considerable attention is 1 Thess 4:13–18. It is a text that is often appropriately used for funeral services. Here Paul comforts and encourages the Thessalonians about those Christians who had died before the Lord's return. This indicates that, for

Ancient Corinth

great opposition' (1 Thess 2:3), and they had suffered from their own countrymen in a similar fashion to the Christians in Judea who were rejected by their own people.(1 Thess 2:14)

In the light of their faithfulness, in 1 Thess 2:20, Paul praises them as his 'glory and joy' with an evident sense of pride that emerges in the first two chapters. It appears that after establishing the community in Thessalonica, Paul moved south to Athens but, due to his thing entirely to live in a manner that distinguished them from the world around them as they waited for the return of the Lord. Paul calls them to base their behaviour on love (1 Thess 4:9), and to 'live quietly, to mind your own affairs, and to work with your hands, as we charged you; so that you may command respect of outsiders and be dependent on nobody.'(1 Thess 4:11–12) Working as a tent-maker/leather-worker was a key element of Paul's own missionary practice, this first generation of Christians, there was a very highly developed expectation that the Lord Jesus was going to return at any moment. As 1 Thess 5:1 aptly describes it, it will come 'like a thief in the night.'

One can imagine the dismay and shock for these first Christians when members of the community died who had been baptized into the life, death and resurrection of Jesus. Paul promptly goes on the front foot and assures them that those who have died will not be

Catacombs of Saint Paul, Syracuse, Sicily

disadvantaged in any way, in fact, the opposite is true: with them rising first (1 Thess 4:16) followed by those still alive going to meet the Lord in the air. That early Christians took Jesus impending return seriously is shown in 2 Thess 3:11–12, where Christians who had given up work and depended on others to provide for their physical needs for a helmet, the hope of salvation.'(1 Thess 5:8) In the face of persecution and other challenges, the Thessalonians are encouraged to 'Rejoice always, pray constantly, give thanks in all circumstances; for this is the will of God in Christ Jesus for you.'(1 Thess 5:16–18) These words of Paul retain a freshness and power that has not dimmed

Philemon

Letters written in captivity

The letter written to Philemon is the shortest of Paul's letters, but it is by no means any the less interesting. It provides a fascinating window into the very real problems that needed to be addressed by the

> ²³Are they ministers of Christ? I am talking like a madman—I am a better one: with far greater labours, far more imprisonments, with countless floggings, and often near death.
> 2 CORINTHIANS 11.23

are strongly challenged. The advice given in 2 Thess 3:10 is powerful, simple and eminently practical: 'if any one will not work, let him not eat.'

What follows in the last chapter of the letter is a powerful reminder to be ready and waiting for that longed for day, dressed with 'the breastplate of faith and love, and with the passing of nearly two thousand years of Christian living. It was by means of their Christian commitment, lived according to this vision, that they were able to face persecution, trials and tribulations, ready to meet the Lord on His return with confidence and hope.

first generations of Christians where both masters and their slaves became Christians. In this particular instance, Onesimus has been with Paul and Timothy attending to him in his imprisonment while Paul awaited sentencing and punishment. While the precise details of Onesimus' coming to Paul are not stated, it is difficult to imagine Paul

needing to write in the manner that he does if Onesimus had been sent to Paul by Philemon. Even if Philemon had sent Onesimus initially, it would seem that, at the very least, he has chosen to stay much longer than his master intended.

Runaway slaves in the Roman empires remained the property of their masters and could not be sold to anyone else. It was the role of *Fugitivarii* to track down runaway slaves and bring them back to their households. Such slaves had the abbreviation FUG branded on their foreheads, and often had bones broken as a punishment. In the light of this practice we can understand the difficult position that Paul finds himself in. He has no legal right to claim anything and this is supported by his statement: 'I preferred to do nothing without your consent, in order that your good deed might be voluntary and not something forced.'(Philemon 14) The fact of the matter is that it is only as a fellow Christian that Paul has any claim at all. It looks as though some financial loss has been incurred by Philemon. This is suggested by the phrase that follows a few verses later: 'If he has wronged you in any way, or owes you anything, charge that to my account.'(Philemon 18)

Ultimately, Paul's aim is to ensure that when Onesimus returns to his master that he will be received 'no longer as a slave but more than a slave, a beloved brother—especially to me but how much more to you, both in the flesh and in the Lord.'(Philemon 16) It is hard for us to imagine how challenging it was for these first Christians to work out what it meant to be a part of a new humanity where the normally accepted structures of masters and slaves—such an essential element of the empire—were now challenged. It was all very well for Paul to state 'There is no longer Jew or Greek, there is no longer slave or free, there is no longer male and female; for all of you are one in Christ Jesus' (Gal 3:28), but it was another matter entirely to deal with the legal consequences of an instance of a runaway slave in a world that did not accept this Christian vision of equality. As 1 Cor 7:21 shows, Paul was not setting out to start a revolution: 'Were you a slave when called? Do not be concerned about it. Even if you can gain your freedom, make use of your present condition now more than ever.' The reason for this advice is that he understood that the Lord was going to return in the near future, and that it was best to live peacefully until that moment. It was only natural that many slaves would desire their freedom, but matters are seldom as black and white as we would imagine and, surprising as it may sound, in the Roman Empire some slaves had more security and benefits than if they were free without employment and lodging.

1-2 Corinthians

1 Corinthians written from Ephesus (Approx. 56–57 AD)

2 Corinthains written from Macedonia (Approx. 57 AD)

The letters written to the Corinthian house churches cover such a wide range of issues that one is confronted by almost too many choices as to where to begin! Corinth was a wealthy and cosmopolitan city in the time of Paul. Having being destroyed by the Romans in 146 BCE, it was rebuilt by Julius Caesar in 44 BCE. Strategically located, it controlled land trade to the north and south, and sea traffic from the east and west. Sea travel was dangerous and Corinth provided a short cut through calmer waters for trade and travel to Italy. Ships would be unloaded and their cargo transported across the *isthmus*, the strip of land between the Gulf of Corinth and the Saronic Gulf, before being reloaded. This provided Corinth with great wealth, and so when we learn in Rom 16:23 that the city treasurer Erastus became a Christian and a co-worker of Paul one can only wonder at Paul's success. Corinth was a city that was dynamic, polytheistic, successful, and hosting an ancient Olympic-type event—the Isthmian games—every two years.

Given the nature of the city, it is no surprise that Paul saw this as a strategic base for his apostolic mission, and why the community so beloved by Paul provided him with so much grief! Paul's relationship with the community was not always an easy one for either Paul or the community. It was one thing to establish a community and move on to other mission fields; it was another thing entirely to address—by means of visits and letters—the sorts of conflicts and differences of opinion and belief that threatened to tear the Corinthian household churches apart.

1 Corinthians is a letter written in response to advice that had been requested by some members of the community, and also after hearing reports from Chloe's people about what was happening in the community.(1 Cor 1:11) The first four

chapters address the question of competition based on personal allegiance to Paul, Peter, or Apollos.(1 Cor 1:12) Paul was deeply troubled by this competition that was so destructive of the fabric of the community. The picture that emerges is of various house churches that were aligned with whoever had baptized the members, or whose style of leadership and preaching they preferred. For Paul, this was a great scandal and his response was to remind them of their unity in the Crucified Jesus who showed what was the wisdom and power of God, in contrast with their all-too-worldly understanding.

1 Cor 1:18 reminds the Corinthians not only of Paul's mission, but theirs too, namely, 'to preach the gospel, and not with eloquent wisdom, lest the cross of Christ be emptied of its power.' For a community that prided itself on its new-found spiritual maturity, it would have come as a jolt to be told that they were, in fact, just 'babes in Christ.'(1 Cor 3:1) Paul reminds them forcefully of just how far they still have to go when he observes: 'For who sees anything different in you?' In other words, while they are meant to be God's Temple (1 Cor 3:16), their division and competition makes them appear no different to anyone else in the world around them. As far as Paul was concerned, the division in

the community was both mistaken and misguided. Both Apollos and Paul contributed to God's enterprise to bring about growth in the community. As he expressed clearly: 'I planted, Apollos watered, but God gave the growth.'(1 Cor 3:6)

It seems that some members of the community totally misunderstood the meaning of their baptism as a license to justify immoral behaviour. In 1 Cor 5–6 this was manifested by one man marrying his step mother, and Paul labels this as immorality of a kind that was not even found among pagans.(1 Cor 5:1) The community was called to bring this person to his senses by temporarily excluding them and sending him back into society. The language that is used is that of delivering the man over to Satan (1 Cor 5:5), that is, back into the world.

To make matters worse, some community members were taking others to court (1 Cor 6:1–8), and others misunderstood their spiritual status to mean they could have intercourse with prostitutes!(1 Cor 6:12–20) We can hear echoes of their slogans in 1 Cor 12:1 where they are saying: 'All things are lawful for me', to which Paul provides the rejoinder that not all things are helpful. Modern readers may well scratch their heads in horror and amazement wondering how they could get it all so wrong. It needs to be understood that they believed

that the body was just a shell, a container for the spirit, and that at death the soul's connection with the body was severed so that the spirit would continue. It was not a long step for them to then conclude that if the body was irrelevant, that satisfying its urges was also spiritually irrelevant.

This frame of reference in which there was an overly developed focus on the soul at the expense of the whole human person helps us to understand why, in 1 Cor 7, sexual abstinence in marriage was the next problem Paul needed to address. It seems that there were married Christians who wanted to prepare for the return of the Lord by trying to live as angels, devoting themselves totally to prayer. Paul had some sympathy with their position, but reminded them that both husbands and wives have obligations and responsibilities. (1 Cor 7:1–4) The more moderate approach he advocates is to refrain from sexual activity in marriages 'by agreement, for a season, that you may devote yourselves to prayer; but then come together again, lest Satan tempt you through a lack of self-control.'(1 Cor 7:5)

It should be kept in mind that the context for Paul's advice on marriage here is that of determining the most appropriate way of preparing for Jesus' impending return. This is the context in which to understand Paul's mysterious phrase, 'in view of the present distress' in 1 Cor 7:26 that underlies his advice to slaves and those who are betrothed to be married. The very practical and real dilemma they faced was how to live while waiting for the Lord's return. Some Corinthians took the line of satisfying their bodily desires in immoral ways, judging the body to be disposable; others took the line that living as angels was the best approach. Paul's advice reveals that he was not happy with either approach. Paul understood all human existence was embodied, and that any attempt to play off one dimension at the cost of another was doomed to failure, even in the short term. Understanding Paul's advice within this context helps us to avoid judging his advice too harshly from the perspective of the twenty-first century. At the time his advice was given, they did not expect that it would be too long before the Lord's return. Paul did not have access to a crystal ball that could inform him that his advice on marriage would still be referred to some two thousand years later!

In 1 Cor 8–10, Paul responds to Corinthians who had asked whether Christians could eat unused meat that was available for sale from the pagan Temples, or whether they could partake in the partly social, partly religious activities that accompanied the sacrifices in pagan Temples. Some of the community were deeply troubled about whether one could be a Christian and be part of pagan worship. Paul understood the position of those Christians who believed that idols did not exist (1 Cor 8:4), and he agreed with them, but his advice is based on love, not knowledge. As he begins to address these issues, he reminds them that while knowledge puffs up, it is love that builds up.(1 Cor 8:1) He uses his own practice of refraining from exercising the right to accept financial support (cf. 1 Cor 9) to suggest that the community should follow this example. In concluding his argument, he calls them to follow his example where he works in such a way as to 'try and please all people in everything, not seeking my own advantage, but that of many, that they may all be saved.'(1 Cor 10:33) At the heart of his argument is that even the least of the community needs to be respected since they are a brother or sister 'for whom Christ died'.(1 Cor 8:11)

1 Cor 11–14 deals with problems in the Christian assembly that can be traced back to a lack of respect for each other, and for a misplaced sense of the need for competition. Given that the society of the time was one where people naturally competed for honour, it is no surprise that when they came to worship they competed for the best seats, argued about whose spiritual gifts were more valuable, and reinforced the differences between the rich and the poor in the community. All of this Paul rightly saw to be destructive, and countered it with a treatise on love in 1 Cor 1:1–13. The only things that will last will be faith, hope and love: '...and the greatest of these is love.' (1 Cor 13:13)

As if there had not already been enough issues to be addressed, 1 Cor 15 deals with a group of people in Corinth who believed that, by virtue of their baptism into the death and resurrection of Jesus, they were already in their resurrected bodies! The argumentation in chapter 15 is dense, and follows along the accepted lines for arguing a thesis in this period. Paul is more than aware that these Christians have not yet come to understand that in order to fully participate in the risen life of Jesus

some radical transformation of their bodies would be required. His understanding is that it will happen in a moment of time.(1 Cor 15:52) The foundation of the argument in this chapter is that the tradition that had been handed on by eye-witnesses is that Jesus died (physically), was buried (physically), and was raised (physically).(1 Cor 15:3–4) Paul uses a number of examples to support his case, but in 1 Cor 15:50 he makes his contention clear, 'What I am saying, brothers and sisters, is this: flesh and blood cannot inherit the kingdom of God, nor does the perishable inherit the imperishable.' He goes on to argue in 1 Cor 15:42 that: 'What is sown is perishable, what is raised is imperishable.' Since they are yet to die it is impossible that they have already gone through the necessary transformation. Whatever the Corinthians may think or believe they are not yet in their resurrected bodies.

As the letter concludes in 1 Cor 16, Paul provides advice regarding the collection that he is administering for the poor Christians of Judea. This project is mentioned in passing in Rom 15:25–28, and most extensively in 2 Cor 8–9. It was a gesture of good will on the part of the Gentile communities in Galatia, Macedonia and Corinth and aimed at material assistance and relief, as well as addressing the fears and concerns the Jewish Christian communities had with regard to the acceptance of Gentiles as fellow Christians. Paul says in Gal 2:10, it was Peter and James in Jerusalem who made the request 'that we remember the poor, which was actually what I was eager to do.'

At the time of writing 1 Corinthians, Paul's intention was to visit Corinth, continue on to Macedonia, and then visit Corinth again. As he describes it, 'I wanted to visit you on my way to Macedonia, and to come back to you from Macedonia and have you send me on to

Temple of Apollo in Ancient Corinth, Greece

Judea.'(2 Cor 1:16) Unfortunately for Paul, and for the community, the first visit did not go well, and it appears that some of the individuals and factions in Corinth were less than pleased with Paul's position on a number of issues, and opposed him. Angry, disappointed and hurt, Paul left the community not returning as intended, but went on to Troas in Asia Minor having written a severe letter that was entrusted to Titus to deliver.(2 Cor 2:12)

This letter achieved a change of heart on the part of the majority of the community, although it must have come at some considerable cost to the relationship because chapters 1–7 of 2 Corinthians are basically a letter of reconciliation, where Paul tries to rebuild his relationship with the Corinthians. In the midst of the confusion, disappointment and hurt, Paul shares with the Corinthians his understanding of his apostolic mission; this provides the context for understanding his reflections on his ministry as a triumphal procession (2 Cor 2:14), and that profoundly personal sharing of himself as carrying a treasure in earthen vessels. (2 Cor 4:7–12) The tone in this section is clearly conciliatory and this is evident in the call to accept the person who opposed Paul back into the community, asking them to 'forgive and console him, so that he may not be overwhelmed by excessive sorrow.'(2 Cor 2:7)

Having reconciled himself to the community, Paul was now able to return to the administration of the collection for the poor in Jerusalem in 2 Cor 8–9. It is fascinating to see that most of the strategies that are used to increase people's contribution to their local church community are already used by Paul in these chapters! He plays the Macedonian communities off against the Corinthians (2 Cor 8:1–4), provides scriptural arguments, such as God loves a cheerful giver in 2 Cor 9:7, and reminds the Corinthians that future rewards will be connected in some way to present generosity. (2 Cor 9:6)

DID YOU KNOW?

While Paul mentions suffering from a thorn in the flesh, no one is sure what he means! (2 Cor 12:7–9):

'...even considering the exceptional character of the revelations. Therefore, to keep me from being too elated, a thorn was given me in the flesh, a messenger of Satan to torment me, to keep me from being too elated. Three times I appealed to the Lord about this, that it would leave me, but he said to me, "My grace is sufficient for you, for power is made perfect in weakness."'

Anyone who reads 2 Corinthians notices the abrupt change of tone that marks 2 Cor 10–13. Where 2 Cor 1–9 were conciliatory now the tone is defensive: it appears the relationship between Paul and his converts is threatened by a new group of Jewish Christians who challenge his authority. They claim 'His letters are weighty and strong, but his bodily presence is weak, and his speech contemptible' (2 Cor 10:10). In 2 Cor 11:22–23, a profile of his opponents emerges as he challenges in return:

Are they Hebrews? So am I. Are they Israelites? So am I. Are they descendants of Abraham? So am I. Are they ministers of Christ? I am talking like a madman—I am a better one: with far greater labours, far more imprisonments, with countless floggings, and often near death.

It is evident that Paul and his opponents are contesting for the honour of being the spiritual leaders of the community. In the midst of what is known as his 'fool's speech', Paul defends his integrity and reflects on the power of God that shines through his weakness. In 2 Cor 12:9 the Corinthians are reminded of what he has learned about the need for humility in dealing with his own thorn in the flesh. God reminded him, 'My grace is sufficient for you, for power is made perfect in weakness. So, I will boast all the more gladly of my weaknesses, so that the power of Christ may dwell in me.' As the letter draws to a close Paul speaks very personally of his fears as he prepares to visit this community again when he says that, 'I fear that when I come, I may find you not as I wish, and that you may find me not as you wish; I fear that there may perhaps be quarrelling, jealousy, anger, selfishness, slander, gossip, conceit, and disorder.'(2 Cor 12:20)

If it had not been for the

obvious human weaknesses of both Paul and his Corinthian converts, then the scriptures would have been that much poorer. In the midst of human limitation—even better, *because of it*—we have Paul's reflections on human weakness, the example of Christ Jesus, and the nature of the apostolate that have shaped countless generations of Christians. We are indebted to the Corinthians: if they had been without challenges and problems, Paul would not have had to write these powerful and profound reflections that have served us all so well.

Philippians

Written in captivity from Ephesus, Cicera or Rome (Approx. 56 AD)

The letter to the Philippians was written when Paul was in prison. It remains a matter of debate as to where it was written, with suggestions ranging from Caesarea to Rome. There is mention of the imperial guard in Phil 1:13—and Phil 4:22 makes mention of Christians who are part of the emperor's household—which indicates that it would have been in a city of some administrative significance, but that leaves open a number of possible locations.

Whatever the outcome of that discussion, it is clear that Paul's imprisonment provided the opportunity to write this letter of thanksgiving, support and friendship to a community that he describes in Phil 4:1 as 'his joy and crown.' It is clear that this community in Macedonia was one that was precious to him, and that he valued them greatly. 'It is right for me to think this way about all of you, because you hold me in your heart, for all of you share in God's grace with me, both in my imprisonment and in the defence and confirmation of the gospel.'(Phil 1:7) Despite his imprisonment, Paul was confident that matters would turn out well: 'for I know that through your prayers and the help of the Spirit of Jesus Christ this will turn out for my deliverance.'(Phil 1:19) Such a phrase may sound like wishful thinking, but it highlights the difference between modern prisons and ancient ones. In the Roman Empire, one was held in prison while waiting for the punishment to be determined, rather than a term in prison itself being the punishment.

As Paul pondered his situation he wrestled with a dilemma: whether it was better to die for the sake of the Gospel, or to remain alive, continuing to support and instruct his communities. 'I am hard pressed between the two: my desire is to depart and be with Christ, for that is far better; but to remain in the flesh is more necessary for you.'(Phil 1:23–24) The community was encouraged by Paul to remain steadfast in the face of opposition they both shared since 'you are having the same struggle that you saw I had and now hear that I still have.'(Phil 1:30)

In a context of opposition, imprisonment and suffering, it comes as no surprise that Paul's mind turns to the sufferings of Jesus as the basis for the life that should characterize the life of Christians-

> [24] Five times I have received from the Jews the forty lashes minus one. [25] Three times I was beaten with rods. Once I received a stoning.
> 2 Cor. 11:24–25

Prison in Phillipi

in-community. The early Christian hymn preserved in Phil 2:5–11 expresses the values of self-giving service and humility that were exemplified in Jesus, who did not cling to his equality with God but emptied himself to the point of accepting death on a cross. Whether Paul wrote the hymn or not is not clear, but it is fascinating to see how early in the life of the community the scandalous death of Jesus was not brushed under the carpet but pondered and explored as the model for all Christian living.

In Phil 2:24, Paul expresses his intent to come to visit the Philippians and in the meantime he recommends his trusted co-workers Timothy and Epaphroditus. That Paul valued them is indicated by his praise of Timothy: 'But Timothy's worth you know, how like a son with a father he has served with me in the work of the gospel.'(Phil 2:22) The recommendation of Epaphroditus is similarly strong, describing him as 'my brother and co-worker and fellow soldier, your messenger and minister to my need.'(Phil 2:25) Epaphroditus had become gravely ill as a consequence of his missionary activity and the community are called to: 'Welcome him then in the Lord with all joy, and honour such people.'(Phil 2:29)

By chapter three the tone of the letter changes somewhat with Paul addressing the question of how the Philippians should respond to those who have come among the community recommending that Gentile Christians should be circumcised. Paul's response is characteristically direct in Phil 3:2; 'Beware of the dogs, beware of the evil workers, beware of those who mutilate the flesh!' Paul goes on to reflect on his own experience and suggests that his own example should shed some light on how the Philippians should deal with this issue. He describes himself as one who was:

...circumcised on the eighth day, a member of the people of Israel, of the tribe of Benjamin, a Hebrew born of Hebrews; as to the law, a Pharisee; as to zeal, a persecutor of the church; as to righteousness under the law, blameless. Yet whatever gains I had, these I have come to regard as loss because of Christ. More than that, I regard everything

Via Egnatia at Philippi

as loss because of the surpassing value of knowing Christ Jesus my Lord. For his sake I have suffered the loss of all things, and I regard them as rubbish, in order that I may gain Christ. (Phil 3:5–8)

These verses express very powerfully that his encounter with the Risen Lord called for a radical reassessment of his own tradition that he had so zealously observed with love and devotion. For him now there is a new goal: 'I want to know Christ and the power of his resurrection and the sharing of his sufferings by becoming like him in his death.'(Phil 3:10) But it's not just the Jewish tradition that Paul re-evaluated, but also Roman allegiance. 'But our citizenship is in heaven, and it is from there that we are expecting a Saviour, the Lord Jesus Christ.'(Phil 3:20) The community of Philippi had a large number of retired veterans who were given land in Macedonia—as a reward for their faithful military service—situated on the *Via Egnatia*, a road of great strategic significance. In the event of an emergency these veterans were naturally prepared to defend both Rome and their own land holdings. While they would have taken great pride in their citizenship, as Paul himself did, there is now a higher call made on their loyalty as Christians.

As is customary for the latter sections of Paul's letters, a number of matters are finally touched on, such as expressing thanks for help received, encouragement for good behaviour, recommendations of traveling missionaries, and concluding greetings. In Philippians the community is called to keep their sights on what really matters. It is beautifully summed up in Phil 4:8, 'Finally, beloved, whatever is true, whatever is honourable, whatever is just, whatever is pure, whatever is pleasing, whatever is commendable, if there is any excellence and if there is anything worthy of praise, think about these things.' In this way they will be able to shine like stars in the world, as he calls them to do in Phil 2:15. Since Paul is in prison, he relies on the assistance of friends, and he takes the opportunity to thank them once again for their unfailing support on a number of occasions. 'You Philippians indeed know that in the early days of the gospel, when I left Macedonia, no church shared with me in the matter of giving and receiving, except you alone.'(Phil 4:15)

Galatians

Possibly written from Ephesus (Approx. 54–55 AD)

Among the letters of Paul, the one written to the communities of Galatia has an intensity and focus that is unique. The issue that is explored and debated is that of the status of the Jewish law and what is to be required in order for Gentiles to become Christians. When the Galatian communities had been established by Paul, no demand for circumcision was made of Gentile converts. Sometime after the initial period of evangelisation, a group of Jewish Christians made their way to Galatia and were preaching that in order to be saved one needed to follow the requirements of Jewish law and, in particular, be circumcised. It would seem that their message met with a good measure of acceptance among the Galatians. Paul's reaction was (to put it mildly) immediate, sustained and vigorous.

As a matter of convention and politeness, letters in this period normally began with a thanksgiving section.(1 Thess 1: 2–10, 1 Cor 1:4–7, Phil 1:3–11, Rom 1:9–10) In Galatians, this was bypassed; Paul begins by going straight to the heart of the matter indicating his dismay: 'I am astonished that you are so quickly deserting the one who called you in the grace of Christ and are turning to a different gospel.'(Gal 1:6)

The letter is written in the midst of an intense debate and, as far as Paul is concerned, the very integrity of his mission as apostle to the Gentiles is at stake. No quarter is asked or given as he argues why the Galatians should resist any inclination to accept the point of view and practices of his opponents. It is shocking for a modern reader to hear Paul say: 'But even if we or an angel from heaven should proclaim to you a gospel contrary to what we proclaimed to you, let that one be accursed!'(Gal 1:8) It is important to realize that Paul's fiery rhetoric is a response to a challenge to his integrity. In an honour and shame society, his honour had been challenged and must now be defended. The intensity of the rhetoric used can be deceptive, and great care needs to be taken to distinguish between Paul's rhetoric and what these opponents were actually like. Both Paul and his opponents were all committed Christians and all would agree that the message of the Gospel was for all people. Where they disagreed was on what was required to become a Christian and, in particular, the status of the demands of the Jewish law.

Given that Paul's integrity had been challenged, he now had to defend himself, and the first part of the letter is devoted to supporting the claim 'that the gospel that was proclaimed by me is not of human origin.'(Gal 1:11) In defending his apostolic call, and the integrity of the mission, what follows in Gal 1:1–2:14 is the closest we have to a snapshot of Paul's early life in Judaism, call and subsequent missionary activity over an extended period: at least fourteen to seventeen years. Paul goes immediately onto the front foot by claiming that he was more zealous for the Jewish tradition than any of his contemporaries, and that this is proven by his persecution of the Christian movement.

All this changed when God revealed his son to him (Gal 1:16) and gave him a mission to go to the Gentiles. After some three years of initial missionary activity, Paul went 'up to Jerusalem to visit Cephas and stayed with him fifteen days.'(Gal 1:18) After fourteen years, Paul returned to Jerusalem with Titus to speak again with Peter and James; he explains that:

I went up in response to a revelation. Then I laid before them (though only in a private meeting with the acknowledged leaders) the gospel that I proclaim among the Gentiles, in order to make sure that I was not running, or had not run, in vain.
(Gal 2:2)

This indicates that he was concerned to be on good terms with the other apostles, even though their practice with regard to the demands of the Jewish law differed. As the letter continues to unfold, Paul makes it clear that he received approval from James, Peter and John for his mission to the Gentiles. The aim of this is clearly to assure the wavering Galatians that he has a mandate for his mission: not only the personal revelation of God, but also the approval of the leaders of the Jerusalem community. He is proud that 'they gave to Barnabas and me the right hand of fellowship, agreeing that we should go to the Gentiles and they to the circumcised.'(Gal 2:9)

It would seem that they understood this differently to Paul, who took it that he should preach the Gospel to both Jews and Gentiles in Gentile territory, while they understood that he would preach the message only to Gentiles, leaving the Jewish mission to Peter. Matters came to a boiling point some time later when Paul confronted Peter in Antioch for inconsistency since, as he describes it, 'for until certain people came from James, he used to eat with the Gentiles. But after they came, he drew back and kept himself separate for fear of the circumcision faction.'(Gal 2:12) What this indicates is not only Peter's basic openness to Gentiles and some leniency in practice, but that he did not feel he had sufficient justification for his practice when challenged by other Jewish Christians.

This was too much for Paul who strongly resisted placing burdens on Gentile Christians that Jewish Christians were not observing themselves. 'If you, though a Jew, live like a Gentile and not like a Jew, how can you compel the Gentiles to live like Jews?'(Gal 2:14)

Having established his *bona fides*, Paul then comes to the nub of his argument that salvation comes from believing in Jesus and not by works of the law. 'And we have come to believe in Christ Jesus, so that we might be justified by faith in Christ, and not by doing the works of the law, because no one will be justified by the works of the law.'(Gal 2:16)

Paul is not saying that the law does not have a purpose within God's saving plan, but that it is provisional when compared to the role played by faith in Jesus. Paul argues that the scriptures support the view that God will bless the nations through the faith of Abraham who was considered to be righteous

> **DID YOU KNOW?**
>
> **Paul dictated his letters (Gal 6:11):**
>
> 'See what large letters I make when I am writing in my own hand!' This is an example of Paul adding a postscript to a letter. In Rom 16:22 the Christian scribe Tertius adds his own greeting 'I Tertius, the writer of this letter, greet you in the Lord.'

before God prior to the giving of the law on Sinai. 'And the scripture, foreseeing that God would justify the Gentiles by faith, declared the gospel beforehand to Abraham, saying, "All the Gentiles shall be blessed in you."'(Gal 3:8) As far as Paul is concerned, the covenant and promises to Abraham have not been revoked, and are now being fulfilled through the faith of Christians in Jesus, who is seen to be the seed of Abraham, and the means by which these promises would be fulfilled. The covenant with Sinai is interpreted as being a guardian for the people until the coming of Jesus. 'Therefore the law was our disciplinarian until Christ came, so that we might be justified by faith.'(Gal 3:14)

Paul continues by marshalling one argument after another, some of it hard to follow for modern readers not familiar with Jewish rhetoric. A good example is that of the section referring to Sarah and Hagar in Gal 4:22–31 that compares—in a most unexpected way—the two women and their offspring. The heart of the argument is the contention that keeping the law is a form of enslavement. In this particular case it may well be that the example of Sarah and Hagar was one used by his opponents, and that Paul needed to provide an interpretation that countered it by turning it on its head.

By Gal 5:1, Paul's position is clearly stated: 'For freedom Christ has set us free. Stand firm, therefore, and do not submit again to a yoke of slavery.' Once again, it needs to be remembered that, outside of this particular rhetorical context, Paul draws on the scriptures and the Jewish law as a source of wisdom and life. In fact, in this letter, extensive use is made of the Old Testament as a means to counteract the argument of his opponents. As Jesus had answered the question about the heart of the law, Paul urges his readers to see 'the whole law is summed up in a single commandment, "You shall love your neighbour as yourself."'(Gal 5:14) Christians are exhorted to live in accord with the Spirit and this is beautifully and succinctly expressed in Gal. 5:22–23 'the fruit of the Spirit is love, joy, peace, patience, kindness, generosity, faithfulness, gentleness, and self-control. There is no law against such things.'

For Paul, it is by living a Christian life in kindness and compassion that God's requirements will be fulfilled. As he puts it beautifully, 'Bear one another's burdens, and in this way you will fulfil the law of Christ.'(Gal 6:2)

ROMANS

Written from Corinth (Approx. 57–58 AD)

For many people, Romans takes pride of place among Paul's letters; and it is not surprising given its theological scope and majesty, coming as it does after many years of apostolic ministry. Unlike his other letters, Romans was not written to a community that he had founded. A consequence of this is that he cannot claim his apostolic authority in quite the same way.

> Gaius, who is host to me and to the whole church, greets you. Erastus, the city treasurer, and our brother Quartus, greet you.
> ROM. 16:23

Erastus Pavement. This pavement is in Corinth and it indicates that the letter to the Romans was written in Corinth.

As Rom 1:10 makes clear, this is a community that he had often wanted to visit, but had not had the opportunity.(cf. Rom 15:23)

One can imagine how symbolic it must have been for him to visit the community established in the very heart of the Empire. If the name of Erastus in Rom 16:23 is an accurate guide to the location from which the letter was written, then Corinth in a likely candidate, suggested also by the mention of Phoebe in Rom 16:1, who is journeying from the Corinthian household church in Cenchreae. At the time of the writing of this letter, Paul is involved in concluding the administration of the collection for the poor in Jerusalem, and his intention is to finally visit Rome on his way to Spain in order to spread the word of Jesus there. (Rom 15:24) This was a community that was well-established and the challenge that faced Paul was that of providing an overview and convincing presentation of his message and ministry among the Gentiles.

For Jewish Christians, Paul was a figure of controversy and Acts 20:20–21 clearly articulates what was the Jewish Christian perspective of his ministry: namely, that he was teaching Jewish Christians living outside of their homeland to forget about circumcising their children and walking in accordance with Jewish customs and laws. In the light of these suspicions, Paul writes to the Roman Christians in such a way that he can allay their fears, and demonstrate that the message he preaches is faithful to God's intentions and plans for all of humanity. As the letter begins Paul clearly states his position, that the message he preaches 'is the power of God for salvation to everyone who has faith, to the Jew first and also to the Greek.'(Rom 1:16)

The picture that Paul paints of the human condition in the early chapters of Romans is one where both Jews and Gentiles are unable to find their way to God or others. Called to live in right relationship with God and each other, humanity is caught in the web of sin and death. As described in Rom 3:23 'all have sinned and fallen short of the glory of God.'

Despite this predicament, Paul invites his readers to wonder, praise and give-thanks for the generosity of God who, in Jesus, now does for all humanity—both Jews and Gentiles—what we cannot do for ourselves. Now, through faith in Jesus, we are brought graciously into right relationship with God, and this is God's gracious gift.(Rom 3:24)

> ...they are now justified by his grace as a gift, through the redemption that is in Christ Jesus.
> Rom 3:24

For Paul, this is an extremely important part of his presentation to the Jewish Christians of Rome. Whatever they may have heard of him, his message is not intended to diminish the value of the Jewish tradition so much as place it within the larger saving work of God that includes Gentiles as well. As a key part of his argument, Paul uses the example of Abraham who was declared righteous in Gen 15:6 *before* he was circumcised. It is an essential part of Paul's argument to point out that God had promised to Abraham that all the nations would be blessed through him. As he argues in Rom 4:11, Abraham is also father of all who believe *without* having to be circumcised.

In Romans, Paul deals with many significant issues: such as the role of the Jewish law now that Jesus has provided the means for all humanity to be saved on the basis of faith. As Paul describes so powerfully and eloquently, 'God shows his love for us in that while we were yet sinners Christ died for us.'(Rom 5:8) Comparison is made between what had been lost through Adam and what had been gained in Jesus Christ.(Rom 5:15) As the letter proceeds, our old self-under-sin is contrasted with our new self, destined for eternal life. (Rom 6:23)

The struggle to be part of the unfolding of God's new creation is one that calls for deep faith and, until it is fulfilled, all of creation is groaning in one great act of giving birth (Rom 8:22–23). In the meantime, Christians are encouraged to patiently endure knowing that nothing 'will be able to separate us from the love of God in Christ Jesus our Lord.'(Rom 8:39)

In Rom 9–11, Paul provides a theological presentation of how he sees the mysterious saving plan of God at work. He suggests that the rejection of Jesus by his own people is temporary, and that it actually paved the way for the Gentiles. The acceptance of the Gospel message by the Gentiles is argued to provoke the Jewish people to faith in Jesus. Paul makes use of the image of wild branches grafted onto an olive tree in Rom 11:17–25 as a metaphor for

the Church now made of both Jews and Gentiles. He believes that just as natural branches were broken off (the Jewish people who have not accepted Jesus), now wild branches have been grafted on (Gentile Christians). The temporary hardening of the hearts of some in Israel has opened the way for Gentiles; furthermore, it is part of God's plan that they will relent and come back. As he states: 'For if their rejection means the reconciliation of the world, what will their acceptance mean, but life from the dead?'(Rom 11:15) His hope is ultimately that 'all Israel will be saved…'(Rom 11:26)

Paul's letters are jam-packed with deep and wide-ranging theological reflection, but they are also practical and focussed on assisting and challenging the communities to live as Christians with their lives modelled on the example of Jesus. The letter to the Romans challenges the community to live exemplary lives in the world as part of the one body. As the letter continues to unfold in Rom 12:4–8, the people are called on to use their various gifts for the good of the community as a whole, and to base all that they do on love; Rom 12:9–21 is a beautiful reflection on what a life based on love and faith should look like. Paul gives practical advice as to how to address a range of problems that the community are considering, such as obedience to legitimate authorities (Rom 13:1), the payment of taxes (Rom 13:6), and not judging others who have different ideas about what Christians can legitimately eat (an issue he had already addressed in 1 Cor 8–10).

Our behaviour has to be based on a principal expressed in Rom 15:1, that 'we who are strong ought to bear with the failings of the weak, and not to please ourselves'. Paul's hope is that caring for each other in this way all can live in harmony.(Rom 15:5)

The letter concludes with a long list of recommendations of travelling missionaries, greetings to and from various household churches, and those who have shared, in various ways, in the ministry of preaching Gospel. While these verses can be quickly overlooked, they provide a glimpse into the dynamism of the early communities and indicate how close the bonds of a shared faith and friendship were for the first generation of Christians.

Appian Way, Rome

Some Recommended Reading

Brown, Raymond E. *An Introduction to the New Testament*, Doublebay, 1997

Byrne, Brendan. *Paul and the Christian Woman*, Homebush: St. Paul Publications, 1988.

Byrne, Brendan, *Galatians and Romans* Strathfield: St. Paul's, 2010.

Dunn, James D.G. *The Theology of Paul the Apostle*, Grand Rapids/Cambridge, GI: Eerdmans, 1998.

Gorman, Michael J. *Apostle of the Crucified Lord: A Theological Introduction to Paul and His Letters*, Grand Rapids, MI: Eerdmans, 2004.

Hawthorne, Gerald F. and Ralph P. Martin (Eds.) *Dictionary of Paul and His Letters*, Leicester: InterVarsity Press, 1993.

Horrell, David G. *An Introduction to the Study of Paul*, London: T and T Clark, 2006.

Knox, John. *Chapters in a Life of Paul*, Macon, GA: Mercer University Press, 1987.

www.ingramcontent.com/pod-product-compliance
Lightning Source LLC
Chambersburg PA
CBHW061059170426
43199CB00025B/2943